ONCE-A-MONTH COOKING™
FAMILY FAVORITES

ONCE-A-MONTH COOKING™
FAMILY FAVORITES

MORE GREAT RECIPES THAT SAVE YOU TIME
AND MONEY FROM THE INVENTORS OF THE
ULTIMATE DO-AHEAD DINNERTIME METHOD

Mimi Wilson
AND
Mary Beth Lagerborg

ST. MARTIN'S GRIFFIN ❧ NEW YORK

www.stmartins.com

Library of Congress Cataloging-in-Publication Data

Wilson, Mimi, 1946–
    Once-a-month cooking family favorites : more great recipes that save you time and money from the inventors of the ultimate do-ahead dinnertime method / Mimi Wilson and Mary Beth Lagerborg. — 1st ed.
        p. cm.
    ISBN 978-0-312-53404-2 (trade paperback)
    ISBN 978-0-312-60118-8 (comb-bound)
    1. Make-ahead cookery.   2. Frozen foods.   I. Lagerborg, Mary Beth.
II. Title.
    TX652.W567 2009
    641.5'55—dc22

                                                              2009011939

First Edition: September 2009

10   9   8   7   6   5   4   3   2   1

CONTENTS

CONTENTS

CONTENTS

RECIPES AND CYCLES

RECIPE	CYCLE
Adobe Chicken	Gm
Apricot Chicken	B
Apricot–Glazed Pork Roast	B
Aunt Rosalie's Stroganoff	A
Baked Mediterranean Cod	C
Barb's Wild Rice Chicken Curry Salad	Sm
Barbecued Roast	GF
Barbecued Chicken for Buns	D
Barbie's Lettuce Wrap-Up	Sm
Barleyburger Stew	B
Beef and Barley Soup	A
Beef Pot Roast	C
Black Beans and Jasmine Rice	A
Cashew Chicken	GF
Chalupa	B
Chicken à l'Orange	GF
Chicken and Dumplings	C
Chicken Broccoli Casserole	A
Chicken Cheese Chowder	B

The letters in the Cycle column are identified as follows

A = One-Month Cycle A   GF = Gluten-Free Two-Week Cycle
B = One-Month Cycle B   Sm = Summer Two-Week Cycle
C = Two-Week Cycle C   Gm = Gourmet Two-Week Cycle
D = Two-Week Cycle D

RECIPES AND CYCLES

ONCE-A-MONTH COOKING™
FAMILY FAVORITES

INTRODUCTION

*I*f this is the first time you've joined us, welcome to a new life, where you'll have meals on hand without the every-evening stress of what to fix. You're going to save money on your grocery bills and save time in the kitchen, so that you and your family can consistently enjoy together time over delicious, home-cooked meals, and perhaps share meals with others. If this is a reunion with old friends who have enjoyed *Once-A-Month Cooking*, welcome back. You're in for more wonderful recipes and ways to spend meaningful time around the family dinner table.

As you launch into megacooking, we're cheering for you! And here's our promise: we'll do all we can to help you not only realize your goals, but have a positive experience in the process. Whether you decide to cook a month's dinner entrées at once, or two weeks' dinner entrées, we'll expedite your shopping and cooking. And we'll even provide table-talk conversation starters to help you make the very most of that time when you're gathered around the table.

What to Expect

For those of you who are new to the method, Once-A-Month Cooking is a different way to cook. You don't have to be well organized or a good cook to successfully accomplish it. But you do need to expect and plan to

1

- Take a longer-than-usual shopping trip, preferably the day or night before you cook.

- Spend the bulk of your month's food expense on this shopping trip (saving money over the course of the month).

- Cook with a partner for maximum efficiency and more fun.

- Cook half a day for a two-week cycle and a full day for a one-month cycle.

- Love the freedom and possibilities this will bring to mealtimes.

- Enjoy family-building times around the table.

- Take the stress out of having company for dinner.

A Look at the Recipes

The **Recipes** included in *Once-A-Month Cooking Family Favorites* have been selected for their taste, variety, ease of preparation, freezeability, and appeal to children as well as adults. Four of the menu cycles are classic, to use any time of year: two one-month cycles and two two-week cycles. Three additional two-week cycles are more specialized and add variety. The **Summer Two-Week Cycle** is for when livin' is easy, grillin' is big, and picnics are possible. The **Gourmet Two-Week Cycle** is more up-scale fare, on average, than the classic cycle entrées. And the **Gluten-Free Two-Week Cycle** provides tasty alternatives for the person with gluten intolerance. We think you'll find that the recipes in the Gluten-Free Cycle are every bit as tasty as the recipes in the others, and are perfect for the whole family where one or more members must eat gluten-free. As always, the person on a special diet should carefully check ingredient labels.

How to Get Started

If you have previously used *Once-A-Month Cooking*, you will find the same streamlined method with entirely new recipes. If you are new to bulk cooking, you'll want to first select a cycle to prepare and read through the lists and charts that are your tools:

The new **Menu Chart** is your best Once-A-Month Cooking buddy. You will want to download and print a copy at www.once-a-monthcooking.com and keep it on the refrigerator, or taped inside a cupboard door. The more you **use** the Menu Chart, the happier you will be because it will help you

- Incorporate into weekly shopping trips any fresh produce required.

- Select an entrée from your freezer to fit the number of people you'll serve on a given night.

- Cycle through a variety of meats, poultry, and fish.

- Select an entrée for the day that will match your available time for final preparation.

- Write in ideas for what you will serve with each entrée. Following through with this important step will help you creatively use fresh seasonal fruits and vegetables and keep track of items that you will need to purchase on a weekly grocery-shopping trip.

- Check off dishes you have served so you know what you still have to choose from—and when you need to plan your next Once-A-Month Cooking day.

The beauty of the big grocery trip is that you can avoid the need for many stops for "just a few" items the rest of the month. Those impulse trips blow the food budget. But we know that you really, really don't want to get full swing into your cooking day and find you're missing a key ingredient, so we'll help you form a complete shopping list. If possible, plan to shop the day or evening before you cook; you won't have the time or energy to do both on cooking day.

The first step toward this is to check the items that you already have on hand. The **Pantry List** is our guess at items you already have. Check and see, and if you're missing some, add them to your shopping list. We give the quantities you'll need so you can be sure that you have enough of each ingredient.

Your **Shopping List by Categories** helps you whip through the grocery store without a lot of doubling back. Supermarkets predictably display the necessities—meat, dairy, bakery, and produce—along the walls of the store. That means you have to travel aisles of impulse items to get to them! We hope to save you steps and detours.

One caution: If you are a super-diligent shopper who likes to buy meats and poultry on sale, remember that it is not wise to thaw meat or poultry, create an entrée, and refreeze it unless the meat or poultry is cooked before it's refrozen. When a recipe calls for precooked chicken, we often recommend purchasing roasted chicken and deboning it. If you do this, keep in mind for your shopping plan that often supermarkets don't make roasted chickens available until the afternoon.

An asterisk (★) after an item in the shopping list indicates that the item will not be used until the day the entrée is served. When the item is fresh produce, such as a tomato, you may want to delay purchasing it until close to when you'll serve the dish. These items are all listed on the handy Menu Chart so you won't forget to purchase them before they're needed. Incorporate these into a weekly grocery shopping list so that you can continue to minimize trips to the store.

Truly you can navigate through a Once-A-Month Cooking day with just a basic knowledge of cooking skills. If you are an experienced cook, you'll sail along more quickly. Using the **Assembly Order**, you will prepare your entrées in the order listed, beginning with your chopping, slicing, and grating tasks. Don't be discouraged with the time this step takes. Once it's completed, the dishes will come together quickly.

Keep the vegetables, cheese, etc. that you process in Ziploc bags or containers on the counter, refrigerating them if they will be sitting out more than an hour or two. Refrigerate all meat, poultry, and fish that you process (slicing, cubing, etc.) until it will be incorporated into a dish.

Depending upon the size of your family, a two-week cycle with some entrées divided into multiple containers could last for a month.

A Few Days Before Cooking

Make room for the bounty by cleaning out your refrigerator and freezer. You won't need a separate chest freezer, even for a month cycle, if you've cleaned out your freezer before you cook. It's time to throw out those hard knots of mystery food. Purge items from the refrigerator that have passed their expiration dates, and clear space for food you'll need to refrigerate between your grocery shopping trip and completion of your cooking day.

On the Night Before Cooking

At every turn in the process of Once-A-Month Cooking, you'll find that following through with the suggested preparation saves you time and inconvenience. The night before you cook, spend a few minutes preparing your kitchen. Remove from the countertops all appliances, canisters, and décor items that you won't use on your cooking day. Set out all items from the Pantry List on a counter close to the stove. Now add to these the ingredients from your Shopping List that don't need refrigeration. Take a few moments to label freezer containers (see bottom of each recipe). Set them out on a table adjacent to the kitchen where you can sit a few minutes while you prepare entrées for the freezer.

Equipment You'll Need

Finally, get out the basic equipment you'll need for your big cooking day. Depending upon the cycle you choose, they will probably include the following:

APPLIANCES

Crock Pot—Each menu cycle includes at least one recipe to be completed in a slow cooker on serving day. If you don't have one, use a large, covered pot in a slow oven (300 to 325°F.).

Food processor—Banish onion tears by chopping onions, a few wedges at a time, "pulsing" with the processor

Mixer or blender—for combining ingredients

POTS, PANS, AND SKILLETS

Baking sheet—for baking; for transporting to the freezer

Large pot with lid—for boiling soups, stews, pastas

Pizza pan—for baking and freezing

Roasting pan—for cooking meats

Saucepans—medium and small with lids

Skillets—large, medium, and small

BOWLS AND CONTAINERS

Freezer containers—Ziploc bags and containers as described on the Pantry List

Mixing bowls—small, medium, and large; for combining ingredients

MISCELLANEOUS TOOLS

Apron—to save your clothes

Clean sponges, dishcloths, and kitchen towels—for wiping and cleaning up

Colander—for draining pasta and spinach

Coolers and ice—for dividing food, if you're cooking with a friend

Cutting boards—One for nuts, fruits, and vegetables, and another for meats and poultry. Or carefully wash your cutting board before moving from one food item to another (always leaving poultry last)

Fresh breeze—whew! Lots of aromas

Indelible marker—for labeling

Happy, supportive shoes—to save your back and feet

Hot pads (oven mitts)—to save your hands

Kitchen shears—for cutting chicken (wash well after using)

Knives—a selection of sizes. Be careful, okay?

Labels or Freezer Tape—for labeling entrées for the freezer

Ladle—for easy transfer of liquids into containers and freezer bags

Meat thermometer—preferably instant-read, for testing doneness of meats

Mixing spoons—for stirring

Music source—for singing while you work

Spatulas—for lifting and turning

Tongs—for lifting and turning

Vegetable peeler—for preparing vegetables

Whisk—for whipping ingredients

The Buddy System

If cooking in large quantity intimidates you; or if you have young children who will need your attention on cooking day; or if you just want to cook with some company, you have options. You can cook one day at your home, and another day at your friend's home. Or you can cook once and divide the food. If you do the latter, the "away" partner should bring two or three medium-size coolers stocked with freezer "bricks" and/or ice. Don't skimp on the coolant, since you want entrées to stay cold until they reach the other freezer. We've found that really large coolers, when stocked with entrées and ice, may be too heavy to lift into or out of a car.

Here is how we have done this when we cook together at Mimi's: Mary Beth gathers from her cupboards any pantry items that Mimi says she doesn't have, as well as any items from the shopping list that she has on hand, and puts them in a large basket to take to Mimi's. She grocery shops on the way to Mimi's, putting the bags of items that need refrigeration into the coolers in the back of her car. She buys bags of ice when she buys the groceries, and/or uses cooler bricks.

At Mimi's house, MB transfers the groceries from the coolers to Mimi's refrigerator. She leaves the coolers closed, with plenty of ice, close to the kitchen. She sets out the canned and dry goods with Mimi's pantry list items and canned goods.

As entrées are assembled, Mimi and MB decide who will take which entrée. If Mimi, it goes into her freezer. If MB, it goes into one of the coolers, along with any item with an asterisk that will be needed when the entrée is served. Sometimes we package an entrée in two containers instead of one, and each of us takes half of it.

Freezing Tips

Once you get those dishes safely into freezer containers, here are some tips to guarantee good taste and texture when they're ready for the table.

- Use the thicker freezer bags rather than regular food storage bags to avoid leaks and tears.

- Label freezer bags and containers with the following information: Name of recipe, date frozen, and the page number from *Once-A-Month Cooking Family Favorites*, for easy reference on the day you will serve it. Recent reports show that bisphenol A is unsafe for use in food contact applications. SC Johnson does not use BPA in its plastic products, Ziploc Brand bags and containers, and Saran brand wraps.

- Let the food cool to nearly room temperature before you pour it into a freezer bag. Plastic bags can melt if the food is too hot.

- Squeeze excess air out of freezer bags before you seal them.

- Some recipes call for more than one freezer bag. Be sure to label all bags, in case they get separated from one another in the freezer.

- To keep multiple freezer bags together, we suggest the following: If the item in the larger bag is not particularly "gooey," you can slip the small bag into the larger one to freeze. If it is gooey, use a strong plastic clip to keep them attached, or use freezer tape.

- Don't overload freezer shelves; air needs to circulate between them.

- If desired, put plastic bins on freezer shelves so that the bags don't "sag" down between the slats. When they do, and freeze that way, it can be hard to remove the bags.

- Use frozen entrées within six weeks, if possible.

Thawing Tips

- The safest place to thaw foods is in the refrigerator. Allow a full day for thawing, and a day-and-a-half for a large, dense entrée.

- Food can thaw unevenly in the microwave. If you thaw in the microwave, plan to cook the food immediately after it is thawed.

- Submersion in cold water is another safe way to thaw food, and works quickly. Do not leave the food in the water after it is thawed. Refrigerate or cook it immediately.

- Bacteria can increase rapidly in food that is thawed and left on the counter at room temperature.

- Place entreés you are thawing on a dish in case the freezer bag leaks or "sweats." A plastic plate with ridges works great.

Making It Work for You

Keep in mind that the point of Once-A-Month Cooking is to make it possible for you and your family and friends to enjoy time together over delicious, economical, home-cooked meals. We hope you will adapt this method to work for you! One way to do this is to tailor the number of servings to your needs. You'll find that the recipes serve from 4 to 16 people, and there are a variety of serving sizes within each cycle, the average being 5 to 6 servings. If an entrée provides more servings than you will use in a given meal, you have options: You can divide the entrée to get two (or more) meals from it. You can divide the entrée so that you can take a meal to a friend. You can serve it when you have company. Or you can plan to eat the leftovers for lunch, expanding the cost savings from your Once-A-Month Cooking meals.

When adapting your own recipes to the Once-A-Month Cooking method, keep in mind that the following foods tend to not freeze well.

Raw salad vegetables; raw eggs in their shells or hard-boiled; potatoes; gelatin salads or desserts; icing made with egg whites; boiled frostings, or cakes with cream fillings; instant rice; rice, macaroni, or spaghetti when frozen by itself for another use; custard pies, cream pies, or pies with meringue.

Over the years we have heard about many applications people have found for Once-A-Month Cooking. Here are a few. We hope that you will be able to add your own:

- Sharon's parents live in a separate apartment within her home. Often they eat dinner together, but Sharon also packages separate portions for them from some of the meals she prepares with Once-A-Month Cooking.

- When a friend of Kelly's is having surgery or having a baby, she'll give them the book and say "Choose 10 of your favorites and I'll cook them for you." She and her husband enjoy cooking together.

- Beth uses Once-A-Month Cooking to keep the evening meals coming between Thanksgiving and Christmas so she can concentrate on extra cooking and baking.

- Heidi teaches a modified two-week cycle of Once-A-Month Cooking to a single mom's group at her church. She incorporates how to teach their kids math, and how they can save time and money by not catching meals on the run. Lori teaches the moms to think ahead: when they cook one meal, to cook two or three. She encourages them to invite over a friend who has had a bad day and share a meal with them, so that they, too, can get the good feeling of helping others.

As we are well aware from our experience revising and adapting *Once-A-Month Cooking*, and now in writing *Once-A-Month Cooking Family Favorites*, ingredient package sizes change, chicken breasts become bigger and bigger (what are they feeding those birds?!), products come on and go off the market. If you are not able to find an ingredient for a recipe in the book, substitute something you think would work well. If you can't find exact package sizes, use the one closest to what is listed in the recipe.

And if—heaven forbid—you decide you don't really want to try cooking once for the month, we hope these will become some of your favorite stand-alone recipes.

Welcome to the Table

After the shopping, after the cooking, as the days roll along, may you discover that these dishes are an enticement to the table. The aroma of a home-cooked meal, and the sight of a set table, create the sense of anticipation that is the definition of welcome. Add conversation that goes wider and deeper than what happened at work today or who misbehaved, and you will nourish people, build your family, and create good memories for other days.

Additional Resources

For downloadable tools such as Shopping Lists and Menu Charts, an e-Newsletter, and helpful tips from other Once-A-Month cooks, visit www.once-a-monthcooking.com.

ONE-MONTH CYCLE A

*T*ake the family on an international journey with delicious dishes from the American Southwest, Asia, and Africa. Sweet Mustard-Glazed Salmon Fillets and Lime-Grilled Mahi Mahi Steaks give a delicious snatch of catches from rivers and oceans.

Menu Chart for One-Month Cycle A

RECIPE	SERVINGS	MEAT USED	METHOD	NEEDED TO SERVE	SERVE WITH
Spaghetti Sauce	6	Pork sausage	Heat	Spaghetti, Parmesan cheese	
Stuffed Shells	4	Pork sausage	Bake	Parmesan cheese	
Italian Sausage and Spinach Pie	6	Italian sausage	Bake		
Lemon Chicken	4	Boneless chicken breasts	Microwave		
Sour Cream Chicken	6	Boneless chicken breasts	Bake	Breadcrumbs, butter, parsley	
Santa Fe Chicken	4	Boneless chicken breasts	Bake	White wine	
Chicken Broccoli Casserole	6	Boneless chicken breasts	Bake	Breadcrumbs, butter, white rice	
Honey Chicken	4	Boneless chicken breasts	Bake or grill		
Marinated Barbecued Chicken	4	Chicken thighs	Grill, George Foreman grill, or bake		
Sweet-and-Sour Chicken	6	Boneless chicken breasts	Bake	Chow mein noodles	
Creamy Chicken Enchiladas	4	Boneless chicken breasts	Bake	Oil, tortillas, whipping cream, Monterey Jack cheese	
Zanzibar Chicken	4	Boneless chicken breasts	Bake	Jasmine rice, cilantro	
Picadillo Chicken Pizza	6	Boneless chicken breasts	Bake		
Salsa Verde Pork	6	Pork shoulder roast	Slow cooker	Tortillas	

RECIPE	SERVINGS	MEAT USED	METHOD	NEEDED TO SERVE	SERVE WITH
Nan's Indonesian Pork	5	Pork loin	Bake	Pineapple ice cream topping	
Cranberries and Pork Chops	6	Pork chops	Bake	Flour, oil, cranberry sauce	
Pork Chops in Orange Sauce	4	Pork chops	Slow cooker	Orange	
Smothered Burritos	6	Lean ground beef	Bake	Tortillas	
Sloppy Joes	8	Lean ground beef	Heat	Hamburger buns	
Pineapple Burgers	6	Lean ground beef	Grill	Hamburger buns	
Peppered Flank Steak	6	Beef flank steak	Broil		
Old-Fashioned Beef Stew	8	Beef stew meat	Slow cooker		
Aunt Rosalie's Stroganoff	4	Round steak	Heat	Egg noodles	
Beef and Barley Soup	4	Sirloin steak	Heat		
Hamburger Quiche	12	Lean ground beef	Bake		
Minestrone Soup	10	Vegetable/meatless	Heat	Shell pasta cabbage, pesto, Parmesan cheese	
Chile-Cheese Bake	12	Dairy/meatless	Bake	Paprika	
Sweet Mustard–Glazed Salmon Fillets	4	Fish	Bake		
Lime-Grilled Mahi Mahi Steaks	6	Fish	Grill		
Black Beans and Jasmine Rice	8	Beans/meatless	Heat	Jasmine rice	

Pantry List for One-Month Cycle A

Herbs and Spices

Basil leaves: 3 teaspoons

Bay leaves: 4 leaves

Cayenne pepper: ¼ teaspoon

Celery salt: 2 teaspoons

Chili powder: 5 teaspoons

Cinnamon: ¼ teaspoon

Coriander, ground: 3½ teaspoons

Cumin, ground: 6¼ teaspoons

Curry powder: ½ teaspoon

Dry mustard: 2½ teaspoons

Fennel seed: 2 teaspoons

Garlic powder: ⅛ teaspoon

Ginger, ground: 2 teaspoons

Italian seasoning: 1 tablespoon

Marjoram: ½ teaspoon

Oregano leaves: 4½ teaspoons

Paprika: 1 tablespoon★

Pepper

Red pepper, crushed: ½ teaspoon (optional)

Salt

Thyme: ¼ teaspoon

Turmeric: ½ teaspoon

Other

Barbecue sauce: 2 tablespoons

Breadcrumbs, dry: 1½ cups (¾ cup★)

Brown sugar: ½ cup

Cornstarch: 1 tablespoon

Cooking spray

Butter: ½ cup (1 stick) (¼ cup★)

Eggs: 10 eggs

Evaporated milk: ⅓ cup

Flour: ⅔ cup (¼ cup★)

Honey: ½ cup

Ketchup: 2½ cups

Lemon juice: 1 cup

Lime juice: ¾ cup

Mayonnaise: 1¼ cups

Milk: 2 cups

Mustard, Dijon: 7 teaspoons

Mustard, prepared: 2 tablespoons

Oatmeal, quick-cooking:
   2 tablespoons

Olive oil: 1⅛ cups (1 tablespoon★)

Orange juice: ⅓ cup

Peanut butter, creamy: ½ cup

Red wine vinegar: ½ cup

Soy sauce: 1½ cups

Sugar: ¾ cup

Tabasco sauce

Vegetable oil: 2¼ cups
   (3 tablespoons★)

Vinegar, apple cider: ½ cup

Vinegar, white: ½ cup

White wine: ¼ cup (optional)★

Worcestershire sauce:
   5½ tablespoons

Freezing Supplies

20 1-gallon Ziploc freezer bags

8 1-quart Ziploc freezer bags

8 Ziploc sandwich bags

1 9-inch pie plate

1 9×9×2-inch baking dish

2 medium round pizza pans

3 13×9×2-inch baking dishes

1 12-cup Ziploc freezer container

1 10-cup Ziploc freezer container

1 8-cup Ziploc freezer container

Heavy-duty aluminum foil

Wax paper

Indelible marking pen

Freezer tape

SHOPPING LIST FOR ONE-MONTH CYCLE A BY CATEGORIES

An asterisk (★) after an item in the shopping list indicates that the item will not be used until the day the entrée is served. When the item is fresh produce, such as a tomato, you may want to delay purchasing it until close to when you'll served the dish. These items are all listed on the handy Menu Chart so you won't forget to purchase them before they're needed. Incorporate these into a weekly grocery shopping list so that you can continue to minimize trips to the store.

Produce

Almonds, sliced: 1 tablespoon needed

Cabbage: 1 head (2 cups needed)★

Carrots: 4 (2 cups chopped)

Cilantro: 1 bunch (13 tablespoons chopped) (2 tablespoons★)

Cranberries, dried (or raisins): ½ cup needed

Parsley: 1 bunch (5 tablespoons needed) (2 tablespoons★)

Garlic chopped: 1 jar (26 cloves equivalent)

Green bell pepper: 3 (3 cups chopped)

Mushrooms, fresh sliced: 8 ounces (½ cup sliced needed)

Onion: 8 medium (1½ onions sliced, 6½ chopped [13 cups])

Orange: 1 (includes orange zest)★

Red bell pepper: 2 (2 cups chopped)

Zucchini: 1 (¾ cup needed)

Dairy

Cheddar cheese, shredded sharp:
1 16-ounce package (12 ounces needed)

Cottage cheese, low fat: 1 32-ounce carton (28 ounces needed)

Cream cheese: 3 ounces needed

Monterey Jack cheese, shredded:
1 24-ounce package (4 ounces*)

Mozzarella cheese, shredded:
1 8-ounce package (8 ounces needed)

Parmesan cheese, grated: 2 cups*

Pastry shell, unbaked 9-inch pie pan: 3

Ricotta, part-skim: 2 15-ounce containers (21 ounces needed)

Sour cream: 1 24-ounce container

Swiss cheese, shredded: 1 8-ounce package

Whipping cream: ½ pint (½ cup needed)*

Frozen

Broccoli, frozen: 2 10-ounce boxes florets

Corn, whole kernel, frozen:
1 10-ounce package (1 cup needed)

Green beans: 1 10-ounce package (1 cup needed)

Mixed vegetables: 1 16-ounce package (2 cups needed)

Spinach, chopped: 2 10-ounce packages

Salmon: 4 6 to 8-ounce frozen fillets

Mahi Mahi: 6 1-inch steaks, frozen individually

Meats, Poultry

Beef, ground: 5½ pounds

Beef, flank steak: 2 pounds

Beef, round steak: 1½ pounds

Beef, sirloin steak: 1 pound

Beef, stew meat: 1 pound

Chicken: 8 thighs and 35 boneless, skinless breast halves

Italian sausage, mild: 2 pounds

Pepperoni, sliced: 1 8-ounce package (deli section)

Pork chops: 10 1-inch center cut

Pork bone-in shoulder: 3½ pounds

Pork loin: 3 pounds

Canned Goods

Beef broth: 2 48-ounce cartons

Black beans: 3 15-ounce cans

Cranberry Sauce, jellied: 1 15-ounce can★

Chicken broth: 1 32-ounce carton (3 cups needed)

Coconut milk: 1 14-ounce can (in Asian section)

Cream of chicken soup: 2 10.5-ounce cans

Cream of mushroom soup: 1 10.5-ounce can

Green chiles, mild, chopped: 2 7-ounce cans

Green chiles, whole: 1 pound, 11-ounce can

Mushrooms, sliced: 1 4-ounce can

Olives, green, pitted: ½ cup needed

Orange marmalade: 1 tablespoon

Pineapple slices: 1 20-ounce can (includes ¼ cup juice needed)

Pineapple ice cream topping: 1 12-ounce jar★

Red kidney beans: 1 15-ounce can

Refried beans: 1 16-ounce can (1 cup needed)

Salsa: 1 16-ounce jar (1 cup needed)

Tomato paste: 3 6-ounce cans

Tomato sauce: 2 15-ounce cans

Tomatoes, stewed: 1 14.5-ounce can

Tomatoes, diced with basil, garlic, and oregano: 1 14.5-ounce can

Tomatoes, crushed in puree: 1 28-ounce can

V8 juice: 24 ounces

Bakery

14 whole-wheat hamburger buns★

1 12-inch Italian bread shell (Boboli)

Pasta, Rice, Noodles

Barley, quick cooking: ½ cup

Chow mein noodles: 6 ounces needed★

Pasta, egg noodles: 1 8-ounce package★

Pasta, jumbo shells: 1 8-ounce package

Pasta, small shells: ½ cup needed★

Pasta, spaghetti: 1 16-ounce package★

Jasmine rice, uncooked: 1 32-ounce package (3½ cups needed)★

White rice, uncooked: 1 16-ounce package (1½ cups needed)★

Tortillas, flour: 16 large★

Seasonings

Chili sauce: 12 ounces needed

Pesto with basil, refrigerated (deli section): 1 7-ounce package (optional)★

Salsa Verde: 1 15-ounce jar (Mexican food section)

ASSEMBLY ORDER FOR ONE-MONTH CYCLE A

Label freezer containers

Processing

CHICKEN

Put 8 boneless, skinless breast halves, seasoned with salt and pepper, in the oven for 50 minutes at 375°F.

HERBS

Cilantro: Chop 13 tablespoons

Parsley: Mince 5 tablespoons

Vegetables and fruits

Cabbage: Chop ½ head (2 cups)

Carrots: Peel and chop 4 (2 cups)

Green bell pepper: Chop 3 (3 cups)

Green olives, pitted: Chop ½ cup

Mushrooms: Slice ½ cup

Onions: Slice 1½, chop 6½ (13 cups)

Orange: Grate ½ teaspoon zest

Pineapple: Drain ¼ cup juice from canned slices, reserve for Sweet-and-Sour Chicken

Red bell pepper: Chop 2 (2⅛ cups)

Zucchini: Chop 1 (¾ cup)

MEAT

Cut round steak into thin strips

Cube 1 pound sirloin steak

Quarter 8 ounces sliced pepperoni

CHICKEN

Cool the cooked chicken, then complete processing chicken as follows. (If desired, save broth from cooking chicken to supplement chicken broth in recipes.) Cook 8 breasts halves, shredding 1 breast for Creamy Chicken Enchiladas, cubing 5 for Chicken Broccoli Casserole and chopping 2 for Picadillo Chicken Pizza. Cut 7 uncooked breast halves into strips for Santa Fe Chicken and Zanzibar Chicken . Cut 6 uncooked breast halves into cubes for Sweet-and-Sour Chicken.

SAUSAGE

Set out one pastry shell, in its wrapper, to thaw for Italian Sausage and Spinach Pie.

Processing is the most time-consuming task. You've accomplished much!
Now start assembling entrées . . .

Prepare Spaghetti Sauce. Simmer for 30 minutes.

Begin preparing Stuffed Shells. When the Spaghetti Sauce is cooked and cooled, complete Stuffed Shells and freeze.

Freeze remaining Spaghetti Sauce.

Prepare Italian Sausage and Spinach Pie and freeze.

CHICKEN

Prepare Lemon Chicken and freeze.

Prepare Sour Cream Chicken and freeze.

Begin cooking broccoli for Chicken Broccoli Casserole.

Prepare Santa Fe Chicken and freeze.

Complete Chicken Broccoli Casserole and freeze.

Begin browning 6 chicken breasts for Sweet-and-Sour Chicken.

Prepare Honey Chicken and freeze.

Prepare Marinated Barbecued Chicken and freeze.

Complete Sweet-and-Sour Chicken and freeze.

Prepare Creamy Chicken Enchiladas and freeze.

Prepare Zanzibar Chicken and freeze

Prepare Picadillo Chicken Pizza and freeze.

PORK

Prepare Salsa Verde Pork and freeze.

Prepare Nan's Indonesian Pork and freeze.

Prepare Cranberries and Pork Chops and freeze.

Prepare Pork Chops in Orange Sauce and freeze.

BEEF

In a large skillet brown 4 pounds ground beef. You will use this as needed for Smothered Burritos (1 pound), Sloppy Joes (2 pounds), and Hamburger Quiche (1 pound).

Complete Smothered Burritos and freeze.

Complete Sloppy Joes and freeze.

Prepare Pineapple Burgers and freeze.

Prepare Peppered Flank Steak and freeze.

Prepare Old-Fashioned Beef Stew and freeze.

Complete Zucchini and Ground Beef Casserole and freeze.

Prepare Aunt Rosalie's Stroganoff and freeze.

Prepare Beef and Barley Soup and freeze.

Prepare Hamburger Quiche and freeze.

Put your feet up for a few minutes and enjoy a cold drink.
Then, the home stretch . . .

FISH AND MEATLESS DISHES

Prepare Minestrone Soup, simmer for 20 minutes.

While Minestrone Soup simmers, prepare Chili-Cheese Bake and freeze.

While Minestrone Soup cools, prepare Sweet Mustard-Glazed Salmon Fillets and freeze.

Prepare Lime-Grilled Mahi Mahi Steaks and freeze.

Prepare Black Beans and Jasmine Rice and freeze.

Complete Minestrone Soup and freeze.

Congratulations! Run a victory lap through the kitchen,
and through the neighborhood.

RECIPES FOR ONE-MONTH CYCLE A

Spaghetti Sauce

1 cup chopped onion
1 pound mild Italian sausage
1 6-ounce can tomato
    paste
1 28-ounce can crushed tomato in
    puree
½ cup water
1 cup tomato sauce
2 teaspoons chopped garlic
2 bay leaves

1 tablespoon sugar
2 teaspoons dried basil leaves
2 teaspoons fennel seeds
1 teaspoon dried oregano leaves
2 tablespoons fresh parsley,
    minced
1 teaspoon salt
16-ounces uncooked spaghetti*
½ cup grated Parmesan cheese*

Sauté onions and brown sausage in a large pot. Add all the rest of the ingredients, except for the spaghetti and the Parmesan cheese, and bring to a boil. Lower the heat and simmer for 30 minutes, partially covered.

Cool sauce. Pour half into a 1-quart freezer bag, label, and freeze for Spaghetti. Reserve the remaining spaghetti sauce for assembling Stuffed Shells.

To serve, thaw the spaghetti sauce and heat thoroughly. Cook the spaghetti according to package directions. Drain the pasta in a colander. Pour the sauce over the spaghetti. Pass grated Parmesan cheese.

SUMMARY OF PROCESSES: Chop 1 cup onion; chop 2 tablespoons parsley.

SERVES 6

FREEZE IN: 1-quart Ziploc freezer bag

Stuffed Shells

8-ounce package jumbo shells
1 tablespoon vegetable oil
1 15-ounce carton part-skim ricotta cheese
1 16-ounce carton (2 cups) low-fat cottage cheese
1 cup (4-ounces) shredded mozzarella cheese

1 teaspoon salt
¼ teaspoon pepper
1 tablespoon chopped fresh parsley
2 eggs
2½ cups spaghetti sauce from previous recipe
¼ cup grated Parmesan cheese*

Cook the shells according to package directions, adding the vegetable oil to the water. Meanwhile, combine all remaining ingredients except for spaghetti sauce and Parmesan cheese.

Drain the shells and run cold water over them. Allow the shells to cool, then stuff the shells with the cheese mixture. This is easiest done by pouring the cheese mixture into a plastic bag, cutting off a corner, and squeezing the filling into the shells.

Place the shells in a 9×9×2-inch baking dish and pour spaghetti sauce over them. Cover the dish with heavy-duty aluminum foil, label, and freeze.

To serve, thaw and bake in preheated 350°F oven for 45 minutes, covered, uncover and bake 15 minutes more. Pass the Parmesan cheese.

SERVINGS: 4

FREEZE IN: 9×9×2-inch baking dish, heavy-duty aluminum foil.

Italian Sausage and Spinach Pie

1 unbaked 9-inch pastry shell
1 10-ounce-package frozen chopped
  spinach, thawed, drained and
  squeezed dry
1 pound mild Italian sausage
½ cup sliced fresh mushrooms
½ teaspoon chopped garlic
⅔ cup chopped red bell pepper

1 cup water
½ cup tomato paste
1½ teaspoon dried oregano
½ teaspoon salt
¾ cup (6 ounces) low-fat ricotta
  cheese
1 cup (4 ounces) shredded
  mozzarella cheese, divided

Line the pastry shell with aluminum foil. Bake in a preheated 450°F oven for about 6 minutes. Remove the foil and bake another 5 minutes. Meanwhile, thaw, drain, and squeeze dry the spinach. Set aside.

In a large skillet cook the sausage, mushrooms, and garlic until the meat is browned. Drain off excess fat. Stir in the bell peppers, water, tomato paste, oregano, and salt. Bring to a boil; reduce the heat and simmer, covered, for 10 minutes.

Meanwhile, in a separate bowl, stir together the spinach, ricotta cheese, and ½ cup of the mozzarella. Spoon the spinach mixture into pastry shell. Top with the meat mixture. Cover the pie with heavy-duty aluminum foil, label, and freeze, with the remaining ½ cup mozzarella cheese in a small sandwich bag attached to it.

To serve, thaw the pie. Using kitchen shears, cut the center out of the foil, leaving the edge of the pastry still covered to prevent burning. Bake at 350°F for 45 minutes. Remove the foil and top with the mozzarella. Bake a few minutes more until the cheese has melted. Let stand 10 minutes before serving.

SUMMARY OF PROCESSES: Slice ½ cup mushrooms; chop ⅔ cup red bell pepper; thaw, drain, and squeeze spinach dry.

SERVES 6

FREEZE IN: 9-inch pie plate; heavy-duty aluminum foil; 1 Ziploc sandwich bag

Lemon Chicken

4 boneless, skinless chicken breast
  halves
⅓ cup lemon juice
1 tablespoon olive oil
2 tablespoons chopped red bell
  pepper

1½ teaspoons chopped garlic
½ teaspoon salt
¼ teaspoon pepper
½ teaspoon dried oregano

Mix all ingredients and place in a 1-gallon freezer bag, label, and freeze.

To serve, place in microwave-safe dish and cook in microwave on high power for 5 minutes. Baste the chicken with the juices, turn, and microwave for 3 more minutes.

SUMMARY OF PROCESSES: Chop 2 tablespoons red bell pepper.

SERVES 4

FREEZE IN: 1-gallon Ziploc freezer bag

Sour Cream Chicken

2 cups (16 ounces) sour cream
¼ cup lemon juice
4 teaspoons Worcestershire sauce
2 teaspoons paprika
2 teaspoons celery salt
½ teaspoon chopped garlic

2 teaspoons pepper
6 boneless, skinless chicken breast
  halves
¾ cup dry breadcrumbs★
2 tablespoons minced fresh parsley★
¼ cup melted butter★

Mix the sour cream, lemon juice, Worcestershire sauce, paprika, celery salt, garlic, and pepper. Pour into a 1-gallon freezer bag and add chicken, completely coating chicken with the sauce. Label and freeze.

To serve, pour thawed chicken into a 13×9×2-inch baking dish treated with nonstick cooking spray. Sprinkle the top with breadcrumbs and parsley and drizzle with melted butter. Bake in preheated 350°F oven for 45 minutes.

SERVES 6

FREEZE IN: 1-gallon Ziploc freezer bag

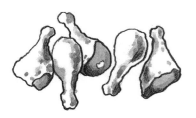

Santa Fe Chicken

½ cup lime juice
¼ cup soy sauce
1 tablespoon olive oil
1½ teaspoons chili powder
1 teaspoon ground cumin
1½ teaspoons ground coriander
3 teaspoons chopped garlic

1 tablespoon honey
3 boneless, skinless chicken breast
    halves, sliced into strips
2 tablespoons chopped fresh cilantro
    leaves
¼ cup white wine (optional)*

Mix all the ingredients together; pour into a 1-gallon freezer bag, label, and freeze.

To serve, thaw and stir in white wine, if desired. Put into a 9×9×2-inch baking dish treated with nonstick cooking spray and bake in a preheated 350°F oven for 40 minutes.

SUMMARY OF PROCESSES: Slice 3 boneless, skinless chicken breast halves into strips; chop 2 tablespoons cilantro.

SERVES 4

FREEZE IN: 1 gallon Ziploc freezer bag

Chicken Broccoli Casserole

2 10-ounce packages frozen broccoli

2 10.5-ounce cans cream of chicken
  soup

⅔ cup mayonnaise

⅓ cup evaporated milk

¾ cup grated Parmesan cheese

3 tablespoons lemon juice

½ teaspoon curry powder

1 teaspoon salt

5 boneless, skinless chicken breast
  halves, cooked and cubed

¾ cup breadcrumbs

1 tablespoon butter

1½ cups uncooked white rice★

Cook the broccoli until almost tender. Drain the broccoli. In a medium bowl, mix the cream of chicken soup, mayonnaise, milk, Parmesan cheese, lemon juice, curry powder, and salt.

Line a 13×9×2-inch baking dish with heavy-duty aluminum foil treated with nonstick cooking spray. Put the broccoli on the bottom. Place the cooked and cubed chicken on top of the broccoli. Pour the soup mixture on top of chicken. Make buttered crumbs by tossing the breadcrumbs in the melted butter. Sprinkle them over the top. Cover with foil, label, and freeze.

To serve, thaw the casserole. Bake in a preheated 350°F oven for 50 minutes. Prepare the rice according to package directions. Serve over cooked rice.

SUMMARY OF PROCESSES: Cook and cube 5 boneless, skinless chicken breast halves.

SERVES 6

FREEZE IN: 13×9×2-inch baking dish, covered with heavy-duty aluminum foil.

Honey Chicken

4 boneless, skinless chicken breast
   halves
Salt and pepper to taste
1 teaspoon dried basil
½ cup soy sauce

½ cup ketchup
⅓ cup honey
¼ cup vegetable oil
½ teaspoon chopped garlic

Sprinkle the chicken with salt, pepper, and basil. Put chicken breasts into a 1-gallon freezer bag.

Mix the remaining ingredients, and pour them into the 1-quart freezer bag. Place the small bag inside the large bag, label, and freeze.

To serve, thaw the chicken and arrange in a 13×9×2-inch baking dish treated with nonstick cooking spray. Pour the sauce over the top, and bake in a pre-heated 400°F oven for 45 minutes. This recipe also grills well.

SERVES 4

FREEZE IN: 1-gallon Ziploc freezer bag; 1-quart Ziploc freezer bag

Marinated Barbecued Chicken

½ cup vegetable oil
⅓ cup red wine vinegar
2 tablespoons sugar
2 tablespoons ketchup
¼ cup chopped onion
1 tablespoon Worcestershire sauce

1 teaspoon salt
½ teaspoon dry mustard
½ teaspoon chopped garlic
Dash Tabasco sauce
8 chicken thighs

In 1-gallon freezer bag, combine all the marinade ingredients; mix well. Add the chicken, turning to coat. Label and freeze.

To serve, thaw the chicken. Preheat a gas or charcoal grill. When ready to barbecue, drain the chicken, reserving the marinade. Place chicken, skin side down, on a gas grill over low heat or on a charcoal grill 4 to 6 inches from medium-hot coals. Cook 45 minutes, or until chicken is fork-tender and the juices run clear, brushing frequently with the reserved marinade. Discard any unused marinade (contains raw meat juices). Alternate cooking methods: Use a George Foreman–type grill, or bake in the oven at 350°F for 40 minutes.

SUMMARY OF PROCESSES: Chop ¼ cup onion.

SERVES 4

FREEZE IN: 1-gallon Ziploc freezer bag

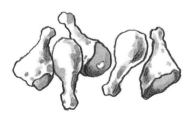

Sweet-and-Sour Chicken

½ cup sugar
¼ cup pineapple juice
½ cup apple cider vinegar
¾ cup ketchup
1 teaspoon soy sauce

1½ teaspoon salt
6 boneless, skinless chicken breast
   halves, cubed
2 tablespoons olive oil
6 ounces chow mein noodles*

Mix the first six ingredients in a large bowl. Brown the chicken breasts in the olive oil. Place the chicken in the sauce and put in a 1-gallon freezer bag. Label and freeze.

To serve, thaw the chicken and pour into a 13×9×2-inch pan treated with nonstick cooking spray. Bake in a preheated 350°F oven for 45 minutes, basting occasionally. Serve on chow mein noodles.

SUMMARY OF PROCESSES: Cube 6 boneless, skinless chicken breast halves; drain ¼ cup juice from canned pineapple slices for the Sweet-and-Sour Chicken.

SERVES 6

FREEZE IN: 1-gallon Ziploc freezer bag

Creamy Chicken Enchiladas

2 tablespoons butter
1 sliced onion
1 boneless, skinless chicken breast
   half, cooked and shredded
2 tablespoons diced green chiles
3 ounces diced cream cheese

Salt to taste
1 cup (4-ounces) shredded Monterey
   Jack cheese*
3 tablespoons vegetable oil*
4 large flour tortillas*
½ cup whipping cream*

Melt the butter in large skillet over low heat. Add the onion and cook until translucent. Remove the skillet from the heat and add the chicken, chiles, and cream cheese. Mix lightly, add salt to taste. Put in a 1-quart freezer bag, label, and freeze. Put the Monterey Jack cheese in a sandwich bag and tape to the larger bag.

To serve, thaw the filling and Jack cheese. Heat the oil in skillet. Dip the tortillas, one at a time, into the oil and fry several seconds until they begin to blister and become limp. Remove and drain on paper towels.

Spoon about ⅓ cup of the filling down center of each tortilla. Roll and set, seam side down, in a 13×9×2-inch baking dish that has been treated with nonstick cooking spray. Moisten by pouring the whipping cream over the enchiladas; sprinkle with the cheese. Bake at 375°F for 20 minutes.

TIP: Cut each enchilada in fourths and use as a hot hors d'oeuvre.

SUMMARY OF PROCESSES: Cook and shred 1 boneless, skinless chicken breast half; slice 1 onion.

SERVES 4

FREEZE IN: 1-quart Ziploc freezer bag; 1 Ziploc sandwich bag

Zanzibar Chicken

1 cup chopped onion
1 tablespoon olive oil
4 boneless, skinless chicken breast
   halves, cut into strips
1 teaspoon ground ginger
1 teaspoon ground cumin
½ teaspoon turmeric

1 14-ounce can coconut milk
½ teaspoon chopped garlic
1 6-ounce can tomato paste
1 tablespoon lemon juice
½ teaspoon salt
1½ cups uncooked jasmine rice★
2 tablespoons chopped fresh cilantro★

In a small skillet, sauté the onion in the oil until transparent. Combine the remaining ingredients, except the cilantro and rice, and pour into a 1-gallon freezer bag. Label and freeze.

To serve, thaw the chicken. Bake in preheated 350°F oven for 50 minutes. Cook the rice according to package directions. Serve over jasmine rice. Sprinkle with the chopped cilantro.

SUMMARY OF PROCESSES: Cut 4 boneless, skinless chicken breast halves into strips; chop 1 cup onion.

SERVES 4

FREEZE IN: 1-gallon Ziploc freezer bag

Picadillo Chicken Pizza

1 cup salsa
¼ teaspoon ground cinnamon
¼ teaspoon ground cumin
2 boneless, skinless chicken breast
   halves, cooked and chopped
½ cup dried cranberries or raisins
½ cup pitted, chopped green olives

¼ cup chopped onion
1 tablespoon sliced almonds
1 cup (4 ounces) shredded Monterey
   Jack cheese
1 tablespoon chopped fresh cilantro
1 12-inch Italian bread shell
   (Boboli)

Combine the salsa, cinnamon, and cumin in a 1-quart bag. Combine the chicken, cranberries or raisins, olives, onion, and almonds in a 1-quart bag. Combine the cheese and cilantro in a sandwich bag. Clip these bags to the unopened Boboli packaging, which can be "bent" to fit the freezer if necessary. Freeze them.

To serve, thaw all the ingredients and place the Boboli on a medium round pizza pan. Spread the ingredients on the Boboli in the following order: sauce, chicken mixture, cheese, and cilantro.

Bake the pizza in a preheated 400°F oven for 16 to 18 minutes, until the cheese is melted and the pizza is bubbly.

SUMMARY OF PROCESSES: Cook and chop 2 boneless, skinless chicken breast halves; chop ½ cup pitted green olives; chop ¼ cup onion; chop 1 tablespoon fresh cilantro.

SERVES 6

FREEZE IN: 2 1-quart Ziploc freezer bags, 1 Ziploc sandwich bag

Salsa Verde Pork

3½-pound bone-in pork shoulder
1 15-ounce bottle Salsa Verde
2 cups chopped onion
3 cups (24 ounces) chicken broth
2 teaspoons ground coriander

2 teaspoons ground cumin
1 teaspoon dried oregano
½ cup chopped fresh cilantro
Salt and pepper to taste
6 large flour tortillas★

Trim the excess fat from pork shoulder. Place the pork in a 1-gallon freezer bag. Combine the remaining ingredients, except the salt and pepper and tortillas, and seal in a 1-quart freezer bag. Label and freeze together. Label the bag with the 6 flour tortillas and store in the refrigerator.

To serve, thaw contents of both bags. Put the pork in slow cooker and season with salt and pepper. Pour the sauce over it, and cook on low for 7 to 9 hours. Shred the cooked pork with a fork. Serve with the tortillas★.

SUMMARY OF PROCESSES: Chop 2 cups onion; chop ½ cup cilantro.

SERVES 6

FREEZE IN: 1-gallon Ziploc freezer bag; 1-quart Ziploc freezer bag

Nan's Indonesian Pork

½ cup soy sauce
½ cup creamy peanut butter
2½ teaspoons chopped garlic
½ teaspoon crushed red pepper
  flakes (optional)

3 pounds pork loin
1 12-ounce jar pineapple ice cream
  topping★

Mix together the soy sauce, peanut butter, garlic, and red pepper and pour into a 1-quart bag. Place the pork loin in 1-gallon freezer bag. Label and freeze.

Thaw the pork loin and sauce. Refrigerate the sauce until serving time. Bake the pork loin, covered, in a preheated 350°F oven for 1 hour and 20 minutes, or until it is no longer pink in the center, or until thermometer registers 170°F.

To serve, stir together the sauce, pineapple ice cream topping, and ¾ cup of the juices from the roasting pan and heat to boiling. Reduce the heat and simmer 5 minutes. Pour the sauce over the pork loin and serve.

SERVES 5

FREEZE IN: 1-gallon Ziploc freezer bag, 1-quart Ziploc freezer bag

Cranberries and Pork Chops

6 1-inch-thick center-cut pork
  chops
1 15-ounce can jellied cranberry
  sauce*

¼ cup all-purpose flour*
Salt and pepper to taste*
1 tablespoon olive oil*
½ cup water*

Label and freeze the pork chops in a 1-gallon freezer bag. Store the marked can of jellied cranberry sauce in the pantry.

To serve, thaw the pork chops. Measure the flour onto a plate, shake on salt and pepper and stir. Coat the pork chops in flour mixture, then brown them in the olive oil in a skillet.

Transfer the chops to a shallow baking dish. Dilute the jellied cranberry sauce with the water, and pour half the mixture over the chops. Cover and bake in preheated 350°F oven for 30 minutes. Uncover. Add the remaining cranberry sauce, and bake, uncovered, for another 15 minutes, basting if necessary to keep the meat from drying out.

SERVES 6

FREEZE IN: 1-gallon Ziploc freezer bag

Pork Chops in Orange Sauce

4 1-inch-thick center-cut pork chops
Salt and pepper to taste
1 tablespoon butter
⅓ cup orange juice

⅓ cup ketchup
1 tablespoon orange marmalade
½ teaspoon orange zest
1 orange, sliced*

Season the chops with salt and pepper. In large skillet brown the chops in the butter. Remove the chops from the skillet, and set aside to cool. Pour the orange juice and ketchup into the pan drippings. Stir, and then add the marmalade and orange zest. Boil 1 minute.

Put cooled chops and sauce into a 1-gallon freezer bag, label, and freeze.

To serve, thaw and pour the pork chops and sauce into a slow cooker. Cook on low 4 to 6 hours.

Transfer the chops to a warm platter. Peel the orange and cut in slices. Slash each orange slice to the center, twist, and arrange one slice on each chop. Pass the sauce.

SUMMARY OF PROCESSES: Grate ½ teaspoon orange zest.

SERVES 4

FREEZE IN: 1-gallon Ziploc freezer bag

Smothered Burritos

Filling:
1 pound lean ground beef
12 ounces (1½ cups) low-fat cottage
  cheese
1 cup refried beans
1 7-ounce can chopped green chiles
¼ cup chopped onion

Sauce:
1 15-ounce can tomato sauce
2 teaspoons chili powder
⅛ teaspoon garlic powder
1 teaspoon ground cumin
3 tablespoons canned chopped green
  chiles

6 large flour tortillas★
1 cup (4 ounces) shredded sharp
  cheddar cheese

Brown the ground beef and drain off excess fat. Add the remaining filling ingredients and heat through.

Divide the mixture evenly among the tortillas. Roll up and place in a 13×9×2-inch baking dish treated with nonstick cooking spray. Mix the sauce ingredients and pour over burritos. Sprinkle with cheese. Cover with foil, label, and freeze.

To serve, thaw the burritos. Bake in a preheated 350°F oven for 40 minutes, or until heated and the cheese has melted.

SUMMARY OF PROCESSES: Chop ¼ cup onion.

SERVES 6

FREEZE IN: 13×9×2-inch baking dish; heavy-duty aluminum foil

Sloppy Joes

3 tablespoons olive oil
2 cups chopped onion
1 cup chopped green bell pepper
1 cup chopped red bell pepper
½ teaspoon chopped garlic
1½ teaspoons chili powder
2 pounds lean ground beef
½ teaspoon salt

¾ cup water
1 12-ounce bottle chili sauce
1½ tablespoons Worcestershire
  sauce
2 tablespoons barbecue sauce
2 tablespoons tomato paste
2 tablespoons quick-cooking oatmeal
8 whole-wheat hamburger buns*

Heat the oil in a large skillet. Add the onion and bell peppers and sauté until soft. Add the garlic and chili powder and sauté for another minute. Add the ground beef and salt and cook until browned. Carefully drain excess grease.

Add water, chili sauce, Worcestershire sauce, barbecue sauce, and tomato paste to the meat mixture, stirring as you bring it to a boil. Lower the heat and simmer, covered, for 15 minutes, stirring occasionally. Stir in the oats and cook 7 minutes, uncovered. Cool the mixture and pour into a 1-gallon freezer bag. Place the hamburger buns in a 1-gallon freezer bag, and tape to the bag containing the Sloppy Joe mixture. Label and freeze.

To serve, thaw. Place the Sloppy Joe mixture in a saucepan and heat through. Serve on toasted buns.

SUMMARY OF PROCESSES: Chop 2 cups onion; chop 1 cup green bell peppers and 1 cup red bell peppers.

SERVES 8

FREEZE IN: 2 1-gallon Ziploc freezer bags

Pineapple Burgers

1½ pounds lean ground beef
¾ teaspoon salt
1 20-ounce can pineapple slices,
   drained, juices reserved for
   Sweet-and-Sour Chicken

⅓ cup packed brown sugar
¾ cup ketchup
2 tablespoons prepared mustard
6 whole-wheat hamburger buns★

Shape the meat into 12 thin patties, using wax paper to press them flat. Sprinkle the patties with salt. Place a pineapple slice on 6 of the patties. Top with remaining patties and press the edges together to seal. Mix the next 3 ingredients and pour into small sandwich bag. Place the patties on a pizza plate and cover with heavy-duty aluminum foil. Label and freeze with the small sandwich bag taped to the top.

To cook, place the patties on a grill or pan-fry on the stovetop. Cook to desired doneness. To serve, spoon on the topping mixture. Serve on toasted hamburger buns.

SERVES 6

FREEZE IN: pizza plate; heavy-duty aluminum foil; 1 Ziploc sandwich bag; wax paper

Peppered Flank Steak

½ teaspoon chopped garlic
1 cup vegetable oil
½ cup white vinegar
1 teaspoon salt
¼ teaspoon pepper

2 teaspoons dry mustard
2 teaspoons Worcestershire sauce
1 dash Tabasco sauce
2 pounds beef flank steak

Combine all the ingredients except the flank steak in a small bowl. Put the flank steak in a labeled 1-gallon freezer bag, pour the marinade around it, and freeze.

To serve, thaw. Remove the flank steak from the marinade and broil 3 inches from heat source for 4 minutes per side. Discard the unused marinade (contains raw meat juices). Slice the flank steak thinly on the diagonal across the grain.

SERVES 6

FREEZE IN: 1-gallon Ziploc freezer bag

Old-Fashioned Beef Stew

1 pound beef stew meat
3 cups (24 ounces) V8 Juice
1 cup (8 ounces) beef broth
½ sliced onion
1 teaspoon Worcestershire sauce
½ teaspoon dried marjoram

½ teaspoon dried oregano
1 bay leaf
1 cup (8 ounces) frozen green beans
1 cup (8 ounces) frozen whole kernel corn
1 cup chopped carrots

Pour all the ingredients, with vegetables still frozen but broken apart as much as possible, into a 10-cup freezer container.

To serve, thaw. Pour into a slow cooker. Cook on low for 8 hours.

SUMMARY OF PROCESSES: Slice ½ onion; chop 1 cup carrots.

SERVES 8

FREEZE IN: 10-cup Ziploc freezer container

Aunt Rosalie's Stroganoff

1½-pound round steak
¾ teaspoon salt
⅛ teaspoon pepper
2 tablespoons all-purpose flour
2 tablespoons vegetable oil
¾ cup chopped onion

2 teaspoon Worcestershire
   sauce
1 10.5-ounce can cream of
   mushroom soup
1 cup (8 ounces) sour cream
8 ounces egg noodles★, cooked

Cut the steak into thin strips, across the grain. Coat the meat with salt, pepper, and flour. Heat the oil in a skillet over high heat. Brown the meat quickly in the oil. Set aside. Reduce the heat to low. Add the onions and sauté until done. Add the Worcestershire sauce, canned soup, and sour cream. Bring to a boil and simmer 10 minutes. Cool, pour into a 1-gallon freezer bag, label, and freeze.

To serve, thaw the stroganoff. Place the stroganoff in a saucepan. Heat thoroughly and serve over cooked egg noodles.

SUMMARY OF PROCESSES: Cut round steak into thin strips; chop ¾ cup onion.

SERVES 4

FREEZE IN: 1-gallon Ziploc freezer bag

Beef and Barley Soup

2 tablespoons vegetable oil, divided
2 cups chopped onion
¼ teaspoon thyme
4 cups (32 ounces) beef broth
1 bay leaf

½ cup quick-cooking barley
1 pound sirloin steak, cubed
1 16-ounce bag (2 cups) frozen
   mixed vegetables

In a large saucepan, heat 1 tablespoon oil over medium heat. Add the onion and thyme, cover the pan, and reduce the heat to low. Cook until the onion soft, about 6 minutes. Add the broth, bay leaf, and barley, and bring to a boil. Reduce the heat, and simmer, covered, until the barley is tender, about 15 minutes.

Meanwhile, heat the remaining oil in a skillet over high heat. Add half the beef and cook, stirring occasionally, until browned. Using a slotted spoon, transfer the beef to a bowl. Add the remaining beef to the skillet and cook until browned. When the barley is tender, add the beef to the soup.

Cool the soup; then pour into 8-cup freezer container, label, and freeze it with the bag of mixed vegetables (still frozen) taped to it.

To serve, thaw the soup and bag of mixed vegetables. Heat the soup to boiling in a large pot and add the vegetables. Reduce the heat and simmer for 20 minutes.

SUMMARY OF PROCESSES: Cube 1 pound sirloin steak; chop 2 cups onion.

SERVES 4

FREEZE IN: 8-cup Ziploc container

Hamburger Quiche

1 pound lean ground beef
1 tablespoon oil
½ cup mayonnaise
½ cup milk
3 eggs
1 tablespoon cornstarch
½ cup chopped onion

2 cups (8 ounces) shredded Swiss
  cheese
Salt and pepper to taste
¼ teaspoon cayenne pepper
1 4-ounce can sliced mushrooms
2 unbaked 9-inch pastry shells

Brown the ground beef in large skillet with oil, drain, and cool. Pour the browned beef into a large bowl with the remaining ingredients, except the pastry shells. Divide the mixture into two labeled 1-gallon bags and freeze. Mark and freeze the 2 unbaked 9-inch pastry shells.

To serve, thaw the bag of ingredients and the pastry shells. Pour thawed ingredients into shells. Bake in preheated 350°F oven for 40 to 50 minutes, covering the pastry edges with foil until last 10 minutes of baking to prevent them from burning.

Makes two pies.

SUMMARY OF PROCESSES: Chop ½ cup onion.

SERVES 12

FREEZE IN: 2 1-gallon Ziploc freezer bags; pastry shell packaging

Minestrone Soup

1 48-ounce carton (6 cups) beef broth

1 14.5-ounce can diced tomatoes with basil, garlic, and oregano

1 cup chopped onion

1 cup chopped carrots

1 tablespoon Italian seasoning

1 10-ounce package frozen spinach

¾ cup chopped zucchini

1 15-ounce can red kidney beans, drained

1 8-ounce package sliced pepperoni, quartered

Garlic salt and pepper to taste

½ cup grated Parmesan cheese

½ cup small shell pasta★

2 cups chopped cabbage★

½ cup prepared pesto with basil★ (optional)

In a large pot, combine first five ingredients. Bring to a boil. Reduce the heat to low and simmer, partially covered, for 20 minutes.

Add the frozen spinach, zucchini, beans, and pepperoni. Heat until warmed through, about 5 minutes. Season to taste with garlic salt and pepper and cool.

Pour the soup into a 12-cup freezer container, label, and freeze with Parmesan cheese in a small sandwich bag attached. Label and store the shell pasta, cabbage, and pesto.

To serve, thaw the soup and heat to boiling. Reduce the heat to low, add the cabbage and the pasta, and simmer, barely boiling, for 20 minutes. Pass the pesto and Parmesan cheese.

SUMMARY OF PROCESSES: Quarter 8-ounces sliced pepperoni; chop 1 cup onion; chop 1 cup carrots; chop ¾ cup zucchini.

SERVES 10

FREEZE IN: 12-cup Ziploc freezer container, 1 Ziploc sandwich bag

Chile-Cheese Bake

1 1-pound, 11-ounce can mild whole green chiles
4 cups (16-ounces) shredded Monterey Jack cheese
2 cups (8 ounces) shredded sharp cheddar cheese, divided
5 large eggs
¼ cup all-purpose flour
1⅓ cups milk
½ teaspoon salt
Pepper to taste
Dash Tabasco sauce
Paprika*

Treat a 13×9×2-inch baking dish with nonstick cooking spray.

Rinse the chiles, split them open lengthwise using kitchen shears, and remove the seeds. (Wash hands after handling and don't rub your eyes.) Dry and drain the chiles on paper towels. In the prepared baking dish, layer half the peppers, half the Monterey Jack cheese, and ½ cup of the cheddar cheese. Repeat the layers. Place 1 cup of cheddar cheese in a 1-quart freezer bag.

Blend the eggs, flour, milk, salt, pepper, and Tabasco sauce. Pour this mixture over top of the layers. Cover the dish with heavy-duty aluminum foil, label, and freeze, with 1 cup cheddar cheese in the 1-quart freezer bag attached.

To serve, thaw. Preheat the oven to 325°F. Sprinkle the casserole with the cheddar cheese and paprika. Bake about 1 hour, or until firm. Cut in small squares and serve.

SERVES 12

FREEZE IN: 13×9×2-inch baking dish; heavy-duty aluminum foil; 1-quart Ziploc freezer bag

Sweet Mustard-Glazed Salmon Fillets

4 6 to 8-ounce frozen salmon fillets
2 tablespoons lemon juice
2 tablespoons Dijon mustard

2 tablespoons brown sugar
1 teaspoon ground cumin
Salt and pepper to taste

Place the frozen salmon fillets in a 1-gallon freezer bag. Whisk together the next four ingredients and pour in a sandwich bag. Add the sandwich bag to the 1-gallon freezer bag. Label and freeze.

To serve, thaw the salmon and glaze. Preheat the oven to 400°F. Season both sides of salmon with salt and pepper. Place the salmon and glaze in a 13×9×2-inch baking dish and turn the salmon to coat with the glaze. Bake until the fish flakes when forked, 10 to 15 minutes.

SERVES 4

FREEZE IN: 1-gallon Ziploc freezer bag; 1 Ziploc sandwich bag

Lime-Grilled Mahi Mahi Steaks

6 mahi mahi steaks (about 1 inch thick), prefrozen, packaged in individual servings
¼ cup lime juice
2 tablespoons olive oil
½ teaspoon chopped garlic

1 tablespoon soy sauce
1 teaspoon ground ginger
1 teaspoon Dijon mustard
¼ teaspoon salt
¼ teaspoon pepper

Keep the fish frozen and place it in a 1-gallon freezer bag. In a small bowl, whisk together the lime juice, olive oil, garlic, soy sauce, ginger, mustard, salt, and pepper. Pour into a sandwich bag and put the small bag in the gallon bag. Label and freeze.

To serve, thaw both the mahi mahi and sauce. Whisk the sauce to combine. Pour the sauce over the mahi mahi in a glass dish. Cover and marinate in the refrigerator for 1 hour.

Place the mahi mahi steaks on a well-oiled grill, and cook until just done, flipping only once, approximately 5 minutes per side depending upon thickness. Brush the sauce on mahi mahi steaks after flipping. Discard any sauce that is not used during grilling (contains raw fish juices).

SERVES 6

FREEZE IN: 1-gallon Ziploc freezer bag, 1 Ziploc sandwich bag

Black Beans and Jasmine Rice

2 cups chopped onion
1⅓ cups chopped green bell pepper
½ teaspoon chopped garlic
⅓ cup olive oil
3 15-ounce cans black beans, drained
1 14.5-ounce can stewed tomatoes,
   undrained

1½ cups water
1 tablespoon red wine vinegar
1 teaspoon sugar
1 teaspoon pepper
½ teaspoon salt
¾ cup tomato sauce
2 cups uncooked jasmine rice*

Cook the onion, green bell pepper, and garlic until tender in a large deep pan, in the olive oil, stirring constantly. Add the remaining ingredients, except rice. Cover, bring to a boil, and simmer over low heat for 30 minutes. Remove from the heat and bring to room temperature. Pour cooled mixture into a labeled 1-gallon freezer bag. Freeze.

To serve thaw the mixture. Heat, uncovered, 30 to 40 minutes, stirring occasionally. Cook the jasmine rice according to package directions. Serve the hot bean mixture over the cooked rice.

SUMMARY OF PROCESSES: Chop 2 cups onion; chop 1⅓ cups green bell pepper.

SERVES 8

FREEZE IN: 1-gallon Ziploc freezer bag

ONE-MONTH CYCLE B

*T*he aroma of hearty simmering delights will greet your family in the evening with this cycle that features slow cooker soups, stews, roasts, and ribs.

Menu Chart for One-Month Cycle B

RECIPE	SERVINGS	MEAT USED	METHOD	NEEDED TO SERVE	SERVE WITH
Chalupa	8	Pork loin roast	Slow cooker	Mozzarella cheese	
Apricot-Glazed Pork Roast	8	Pork loin roast	Slow cooker		
Country-Style Ribs	8	Pork loin ribs	Slow cooker		
Ham with Pineapple Sauce	6	Ham	Heat		
Italian Sausage Soup with Tortellini	8	Italian sausage	Boil	Tortellini, Parmesan cheese	
Egg Bake	8	Lil' Smokies	Bake		
Pork Loin with Sour Cherries	4	Pork loin chops	Bake		
Mediterranean Fish Stew with Spicy Hot Mustard	4-6	Fish: cod	Heat	Mayonnaise, red potatoes	
Chicken–Wild Rice Soup	6	Rotisserie chicken	Boil	Flour, half-and-half	
Pozole Soup	8	Rotisserie chicken	Slow cooker	Monterey Jack cheese, salsa, lettuce, tortilla chips	
Chicken-Cheese Chowder	4	Rotisserie chicken	Heat	Milk	
Melt-in-Your-Mouth Chicken Pie	6	Rotisserie chicken	Bake	Chicken broth, chicken soup	
Mexican Two-Bean Chicken Chili	8	Rotisserie chicken	Slow cooker	Sour cream, tomatoes, tortilla chips	
Jerk Chicken	4	Boneless chicken breasts	Grill or broil		
Jerk Pork	4	Pork loin chops	Grill or broil		

RECIPE	SERVINGS	MEAT USED	METHOD	NEEDED TO SERVE	SERVE WITH
Italian Slow Cooker Chicken	4	Boneless chicken breasts	slow cooker	potatoes	
Southwestern Chicken	5	Boneless chicken breasts	Bake		
Apricot Chicken	4	Boneless chicken breasts	Microwave	Rice	
Chicken Supreme	6	Boneless chicken breasts	Bake		
Garlic-Cheddar Chicken	8	Boneless chicken breasts	Bake		
Ginger-Yogurt Chicken	4	Boneless chicken breasts	Grill or bake		
Quick and Easy Chinese Chicken	6	Boneless chicken breasts	Bake		
Fajitas	4	Round steak	Sauté	Olive oil, flour tortillas, sour cream, salsa	
Pita Sandwiches	6	Ground beef	Heat	Pita bread, tomatoes, cucumber, yogurt, parsley, mint	
Fiesta Dinner	5	Ground beef	Heat	Rice, peas, yogurt, cornstarch, parsley	
Hot Open-Faced Sandwiches	8	Ground beef	Bake	Hamburger buns	
Meat Loaf	6	Ground beef	Bake		
South-of-the-Border Ground Beef and Corn Pie	6	Ground beef	Bake	Ripe olives	
Barleyburger Stew	6	Ground beef	Slow cooker		
Oriental Hotdish	4	Ground beef	Bake		

Pantry List for One-Month Cycle B

Herbs and Spices

Allspice, ground: 4 teaspoons

Basil leaves: ¾ teaspoon

Cayenne pepper: 1 tablespoon

Celery salt: 1 teaspoon

Celery seed: ½ teaspoon

Chili powder: 3½ tablespoons

Cinnamon: 1 teaspoon

Cumin, ground: 4½ teaspoons

Dry mustard: 1 teaspoon

Fennel seed: 1 teaspoon

Garlic powder: 2 tablespoons

Ginger, ground: 1¼ teaspoons

Mint, dried: ½ teaspoon

Nutmeg: ¾ teaspoon

Oregano leaves: 4 teaspoons

Paprika: ½ teaspoon

Pepper

Sage: 1½ teaspoons

Salt

Seasoned salt: ½ teaspoon

Thyme: 3¼ teaspoons

Other

Apple cider vinegar: 3 tablespoons

Baking powder: 2 teaspoons

Baking soda: ½ teaspoon

Breadcrumbs, dry: 1½ cups

Brown sugar: 2 cups

Butter: 1¼ cups (2½ sticks)

Cooking spray

Cornstarch: 2½ tablespoons

Eggs: 16

Flour: 1½ cups

Lemon juice: 2 teaspoons

Lime juice: 1 cup

Ketchup: 2 cups

Milk: 3¾ cups

Mayonnaise: ⅔ cup

Mustard, Dijon: 2 tablespoons

Mustard, prepared: 1 teaspoon

Oatmeal, quick-cooking: ½ cup

Olive oil: 1 cup

Orange juice: ½ cup

Sherry: 1 tablespoon

Soy sauce: 1 cup

Sugar: 2 tablespoons

Tabasco Sauce: 1 tablespoon

Vegetable oil: 2 tablespoons

White vinegar: 1 cup

White wine, dry: ½ cup

Worcestershire sauce:
1½ teaspoons

Freezing Supplies

23 1-gallon Ziploc freezer bags

6 1-quart Ziploc freezer bags

7 Ziploc sandwich bags

2 13×9×2-inch baking dishes

1 8×8×2-inch baking dish

Heavy-duty aluminum foil

1 10-cup Ziploc freezer container

2 12-cup Ziploc freezer containers

1 16-cup Ziploc freezer container

1 Pyrex loaf pan

Indelible marking pen

Freezer tape

SHOPPING LIST FOR ONE-MONTH CYCLE B BY CATEGORIES

An asterisk (★) after an item in the shopping list indicates that the item will not be used until the day the entrée is served. When the item is fresh produce, such as a tomato, you may want to delay purchasing it until close to when you'll served the dish. These items are all listed on the handy Menu Chart so you won't forget to purchase them before they're needed. Incorporate these into a weekly grocery shopping list so that you can continue to minimize trips to the store.

Produce

Carrots: 7 (1 cup shredded, 2½ cups chopped)

Celery: 11 stalks (3½ cups chopped)

Cucumber: 1 small★

Garlic, chopped: 1 jar (31 cloves)

Green bell pepper: 8 (1 cut in strips, 6 chopped [8 cups])

Green onions: 1 bunch (⅓ cup needed)

Lettuce: 1 head (½ needed)★

Lemon: 1

Onion: 10 medium (1½ cut in strips, 8½ chopped [17 cups])

Onion, red: 1 (2 cups chopped)

Parsley: 1 bunch (½ cup chopped)

Potatoes: 2★

Red bell pepper: 2 (1 cut in strips, 1 chopped [1⅓ cup])

Red potatoes: 3

Scotch bonnet pepper: 1 (for less fire substitute 1 green bell pepper)

Tomatoes, fresh: 6 plum tomatoes★ (3 chopped, 3 sliced)

Zucchini: 3 medium (2½ cups chopped)

Dairy

Buttermilk: ½ pint (1 cup needed)

Mild cheddar cheese, shredded:
1 24-ounce package (22 ounces
needed)

Colby-Jack cheese, shredded:
1 16-ounce package

Half-and-Half: 1 pint

Monterey Jack cheese, shredded:
1 8-ounce package★ (4 ounces
needed)

Mozzarella cheese, shredded:
2 8-ounce packages (10 ounces
needed)

Parmesan cheese, grated: 1½ cups

Sour cream: 16-ounce carton★

Yogurt, plain: 3 6-ounce containers

Frozen

Corn, whole kernel, frozen: 1
16-ounce package (2 cups needed)

Hash browns, frozen country-
style: 1 12-ounce package

Mixed vegetables, frozen:
1 16-ounce package

Peas, frozen: 1 8-ounce package
(½ cup needed)

Tortellini, frozen, meat- or
cheese-filled: 1 16-ounce
package

Meats, Poultry, Fish

Bacon: 6 slices

Beef, lean ground: 8 pounds

Beef, round steak: 1½ pounds

Chicken, boneless, skinless breast
halves: 39 breast halves

Chicken, roasted (rotisserie):
4 whole (11 cups shredded
chicken needed)

Cod: 1½ to 2 pounds

Ham steak: 1¾ pounds

Italian sausage, mild: 1 pound

Lit'l Smokies: 1 10-ounce package

Pork loin chops, thick, boneless: 8

Pork loin country-style ribs: 4½ pounds

Pork boneless loin roast:
6½ pounds (1 3-pound roast,
1 3½-pound roast)

Canned Goods

Apricot preserves: 1 11.5-ounce jar

Bean sprouts: 1 12-ounce can

Beef broth: 1 48-ounce carton;
1 32-ounce carton

Black beans: 1 15-ounce can

Chicken broth: 4 48-ounce cartons

Claim juice: 1 8-ounce bottle

Corn, whole kernel: 1 8.75-ounce can

Cream of chicken soup:
2 10.5-ounce cans

Cream of mushroom soup:
2 10.5-ounce cans

Green chilies, chopped:
2 4-ounce cans

Hominy: 2 15-ounce cans (or Great Northern Beans)

Mushroom pieces and stems:
2 4-ounce cans

Olives, ripe, sliced: 2 2¼-ounce cans

Peperoncini peppers: 1 12-ounce jar (4 peppers needed)

Pineapple, crushed: 1 20-ounce can

Pinto beans: 1 15-ounce can

Sour cherries: 1 15-ounce can

Tomato juice: 1 46-ounce can

Tomato sauce: 4 8-ounce cans;
1 15-ounce can

Tomatoes, diced: 1 14.5-ounce can;
3 28-ounce cans

Bakery

Buns, whole-wheat hamburger: 8★   **Tortillas, large flour:** 4★

Pita pockets: 6★

Pasta, Rice, Beans

Barley: ½ cup

Rice: 2½ cups uncooked long grain

Uncle Ben's Original Long Grain and Wild Rice: 1 6-ounce box

Dry pinto beans: 1 pound (2 cups)

Seasonings

Italian salad dressing: ½ cup

Salsa: 2 14.5-ounce jars

Taco seasoning: 1 1-ounce packet

Other

Almonds, sliced: 1 2.5-ounce package (6 tablespoons needed)

Cashews, salted: 1 2-ounce package (½ cup needed)

Red wine, dry: 1½ cups

Tortilla chips: 1 large bag★

ASSEMBLY ORDER FOR ONE-MONTH CYCLE B

Label freezer containers.

Processing

VEGETABLES

Carrots: Peel and chop 5 (2½ cups); peel and shred 2 (1 cup)

Celery: Chop 11 stalks (3½ cups)

Green bell peppers: Chop 7 (8⅓ cups); slice 1 into strips (NOTE: If substituting for Scotch bonnet pepper, chop 8)

Green onion: Chop ⅓ cup

Lemon: Grate ½ lemon for zest

Onions: Chop 8½ (17 cups); slice 1½ into strips

Onion, red: Chop 1 (2 cups)

Parsley: Chop ½ cup

Peperoncini peppers: Chop 4

Red bell peppers: Chop 1 (1⅓ cups); slice 1 into strips

Scotch bonnet pepper: Chop 1

Zucchini: Chop 3 (1½ cups)

PORK

Lit'l Smokies: cut into ½-inch slices

BEEF

Slice round steak into thin strips

CHICKEN

Cut 2 breasts into strips

Pound to flatten 8 boneless, skinless chicken breast halves

Roasted (rotisserie) chicken; debone and shred 4 whole

Processing is the most time-consuming task. You've accomplished much!
Now start assembling entrées . . .

CHICKEN

Prepare Southwestern Chicken and freeze.

Prepare Apricot Chicken and freeze.

Fry bacon for Chicken Supreme.

Cook Uncle Ben's Original Long Grain and Wild Rice according to package
directions for Chicken–Wild Rice Soup.

Prepare Ginger-Yogurt Chicken and freeze.

Prepare Quick and Easy Chinese Chicken and freeze.

Complete Chicken Supreme and freeze.

Prepare Italian Slow Cooker Chicken and freeze.

Prepare Garlic-Cheddar Chicken and freeze (You will use this small skillet
again; when garlic is heated, just wipe the skillet.)

Prepare Chicken–Wild Rice Soup and freeze.

Prepare Pozole Soup, using small skillet you sautéed garlic in, and freeze.

Prepare Chicken-Cheese Chowder and freeze.

Prepare Melt-in-Your-Mouth Chicken Pie and freeze.

Prepare Mexican Two–Bean Chicken Chili and freeze.

Prepare Jerk Chicken and Jerk Pork and freeze.

You have completed nearly half of the entrées! Celebrate!

PORK

Start Italian Sausage Soup with Tortellini in large pot.

Prepare Ham with Pineapple Sauce and freeze.

Prepare Chalupa and freeze.

Prepare Country-Style Ribs and freeze.

Prepare Apricot-Glazed Pork Roast and freeze.

Prepare Egg Bake; wipe out skillet to re-use.

Prepare Pork Loin with Sour Cherries and freeze.

Complete Italian Sausage Soup with Tortellini and freeze. You will be using the large pot again to brown the ground beef.

FISH

Prepare Mediterranean Fish Stew with Spicy Mayonnaise and freeze.

BEEF

Brown 6 pounds lean ground beef in large pot until slightly pink. Drain excess fat. Set aside.

Prepare Pita Sandwiches using $1/6$ of the ground beef and freeze.

Prepare Meat Loaf and freeze.

Prepare Fajitas and freeze.

Prepare Fiesta Dinner in medium saucepan using 1 pound ($1/6$) of the browned ground beef and freeze.

Prepare Hot Open-Faced Sandwiches in a medium skillet using 1 pound ($^1/_6$) of the browned ground beef and freeze.

Prepare South-of-the-Border Ground Beef and Corn Pie using 1 pound ($^1/_6$) of the browned meat and freeze.

In same medium saucepan prepare Barleyburger Stew using 1 pound ($^1/_6$) of the browned meat and freeze.

Prepare Oriental Hotdish using 1 pound ($^1/_6$) of the browned meat and freeze.

You're finished! Run a victory lap through the kitchen,
and through the neighborhood!

RECIPES FOR ONE-MONTH CYCLE B

Southwestern Chicken

1 28-ounce can diced tomatoes
1⅓ cups chopped red bell pepper
1⅓ cups chopped green bell pepper
2 cups chopped red onion
1½ teaspoons chopped garlic
2 tablespoons lime juice
⅓ cup olive oil

½ teaspoon salt
½ teaspoon pepper
¼ teaspoon cayenne pepper
½ teaspoon Tabasco sauce; add more
for spicier chicken
5 boneless, skinless chicken breasts
halves

Mix all the ingredients together and pour over the chicken in 1-gallon freezer bag. Label and freeze.

To serve, thaw the ingredients. Pour into a 13×9×2-inch baking dish. Bake in a preheated 375°F oven for 50 minutes.

SUMMARY OF PROCESSES: Chop 1⅓ cups each of red and green bell pepper; chop 2 cups red onions.

SERVES 5

FREEZE IN: 1-gallon Ziploc freezer bag

Apricot Chicken

½ cup (4 ounces) apricot preserves
2 tablespoons soy sauce
1 tablespoon sherry
1 tablespoon vegetable oil
1 tablespoon cornstarch
½ teaspoon chopped garlic

¼ teaspoon ground ginger
1⅓ cups chopped green bell pepper
2 boneless skinless chicken breast
   halves, cut into strips
½ cup salted cashews
1 cup uncooked rice*

In a 1-gallon freezer bag, combine the first 8 ingredients and the chicken strips. Place the salted cashews in the sandwich bag. Place the small bag in the gallon bag with the chicken, label, and freeze.

To serve, thaw the bags. Cook the rice according to package directions. Combine the chicken with the sauce. Transfer the chicken mixture to a shallow microwave-safe dish. Cover and microwave on high for 3 minutes, stirring once. Add the cashews. Cover and microwave on high for 2 to 4 minutes, stirring once, or until the chicken juices run clear. Let stand for 3 minutes. Serve with the cooked rice.

SUMMARY OF PROCESSES: Chop 1⅓ cups green bell pepper; cut 2 chicken breasts into strips.

SERVES 4

FREEZE IN: 1-gallon Ziploc freezer bag and 1 sandwich Ziploc bag.

Chicken Supreme

6 slices bacon
6 boneless, skinless chicken breast
halves
1 10.5-ounce cans cream of
mushroom soup

½ cup sour cream
1 dash Tabasco sauce, or to
taste

Fry the bacon until crisp and break into pieces. Put the chicken and bacon into a 1-gallon freezer bag. Mix the remaining ingredients and pour into a 1-quart freezer bag. Slip the sauce bag into the bag of chicken and bacon, label, and freeze.

To serve, thaw the chicken mixture. Arrange the chicken and bacon in 13×9×2-inch baking dish and pour the sauce on top. Bake in a preheated 375°F oven for 50 minutes.

SERVES 6

FREEZE IN: 1-gallon Ziploc freezer bag; 1-quart Ziploc freezer bag

Ginger-Yogurt Chicken

4 boneless, skinless chicken breast
    halves
1 6-ounce carton plain yogurt
1½ teaspoons chopped garlic

2 teaspoons ground ginger
2 teaspoons lemon juice
1 teaspoon chili powder
½ teaspoon salt

Mix all the ingredients together and pour into a 1-gallon freezer bag, label, and freeze.

To serve, thaw the chicken. Grill the chicken on a gas grill on medium or a charcoal grill over medium-hot coals until the chicken is no longer pink and the juices run clear. Alternate cooking method: Bake in the oven at 375°F for 50 minutes.

SERVES 4

FREEZE IN: 1-gallon Ziploc freezer bag

Quick and Easy Chinese Chicken

6 boneless, skinless chicken breast
   halves
¾ cup ketchup
¼ cup soy sauce
½ cup firmly packed brown sugar

2 tablespoons white vinegar
¼ cup chopped onion
½ teaspoon chopped garlic
½ teaspoon seasoned salt

Place the chicken in a 1–gallon freezer bag. Combine the remaining ingredients, stir well, and pour over the chicken. Label and freeze.

To serve, thaw and bake, uncovered, at 350°F for 50 minutes, or until the chicken is done, turning chicken over after 30 minutes, and basting occasionally.

SUMMARY OF PROCESSES: Chop ¼ cup onions.

SERVES 6

FREEZE IN: 1–gallon Ziploc freezer bag

Italian Slow Cooker Chicken

4 boneless, skinless chicken breast
   halves
½ cup Italian salad dressing
1 cup chopped green bell peppers

1 cup chopped onions
1½ teaspoons chopped garlic
2 potatoes*, peeled and cut in
   wedges

Combine all ingredients except the potatoes in a 1-gallon freezer bag, label, and freeze.

To serve, thaw and pour the contents of the bag into slow cooker. Cook on low for 7 to 8 hours. After 6 hours of cooking, add the potato wedges.

SUMMARY OF PROCESSES: Chop 1 cup green bell peppers; chop 1 cup onions.

SERVES 4

FREEZE IN: 1-gallon Ziploc freezer bag

Garlic-Cheddar Chicken

2 teaspoons chopped garlic
½ cup butter
¾ cup dry breadcrumbs
½ cup grated Parmesan cheese
1½ cups (6 ounces) mild shredded
  cheddar cheese

1 tablespoon chopped fresh parsley
¼ teaspoon dried oregano
¼ teaspoon pepper
¼ teaspoon salt
8 skinless, boneless chicken breast
  halves

Sauté the garlic in the butter, for about 5 minutes.

In a shallow bowl, mix the breadcrumbs, Parmesan cheese, cheddar cheese, parsley, oregano, pepper, and salt. Pound the chicken breasts to flatten them. Dip each chicken breast in the garlic butter to coat, then press into the breadcrumb mixture. Arrange the coated chicken breasts in a 13×9×2-inch baking dish that has been treated with nonstick cooking spray. Drizzle with any remaining butter and top with any remaining breadcrumb mixture. Cover with heavy-duty aluminum foil, label, and freeze.

To serve, thaw. Preheat the oven to 375°F. Bake, covered with foil, for 45 minutes. Uncover and cook another 15 minutes, or until the chicken is no longer pink and the juices run clear.

SUMMARY OF PROCESSES: Pound 8 chicken breasts to flatten them.

SERVES 8

FREEZE IN: 13×9×2-inch baking dish; heavy-duty aluminum foil

Chicken–Wild Rice Soup

¼ cup butter

1 cup chopped onion

1 6-ounce box Uncle Ben's Original Long Grain and Wild Rice

2 cups deboned and shredded rotisserie chicken

1 48-ounce carton (6 cups) chicken broth

1 4-ounce can mushroom pieces and stems, drained

6 tablespoons sliced almonds

1 cup chopped carrots

¼ cup all-purpose flour★

1 pint (2 cups) half-and-half★

Cook the rice according to package directions. Melt the butter in a large pot, add the onions, and sauté. Add the rice and all the other ingredients except for the flour and half-and-half. Simmer for 20 minutes. Cool, pour into labeled 10-cup plastic freezer container, and freeze.

To serve, thaw the soup and pour into a large saucepan. Bring to a boil, reduce the heat, and simmer for 30 minutes. Just before serving, whisk the flour with the half-and-half in a small bowl. Add it to the soup, heat through until thickened, and serve.

SUMMARY OF PROCESSES: Debone and shred 2 cups rotisserie chicken; chop 1 cup onions; chop 1 cup carrots.

SERVES 6

FREEZE IN: 10-cup plastic freezer container

Pozole Soup

½ cup chopped onion
½ teaspoon chopped garlic
1 tablespoon vegetable oil
2 cups deboned and shredded
  rotisserie chicken
1 48-ounce carton (6 cups) chicken
  broth
2 15-ounce cans hominy or Great
  Northern beans, drained

2 teaspoons dried oregano
1 1-ounce package taco seasoning
1 4-ounce can chopped green chiles
1 cup (4 ounces) shredded Monterey
  Jack cheese★
Salsa★
Tortilla chips★
½ head lettuce★

Sauté the onion and garlic in the oil. Pour into a bowl with the remaining
ingredients and mix together. Pour into the soup 10-cup freezer container,
label, and freeze.

To serve, thaw the soup and pour into slow cooker. Cook on low 3 hours.
Serve with the shredded cheese, salsa, and crushed tortilla chips sprinkled on
top of the hot soup.

SUMMARY OF PROCESSES: Debone and shred 2 cups rotisserie chicken;
chop ½-cup onions.

SERVES 8

FREEZE IN: 10-cup plastic freezer container

Chicken-Cheese Chowder

1 cup shredded carrot
¼ cup chopped onion
2 tablespoons butter
¼ cup all-purpose flour
2 cups chicken broth
1 cup deboned and shredded
  rotisserie chicken
1 4-ounce can mushroom pieces and
  stems

3 tablespoons dry white wine
  (optional)
1 teaspoon celery salt
½ teaspoon Worcestershire
  sauce
2 cups (8 ounces) shredded mild
  cheddar cheese
2 cups milk★

In large skillet, sauté the carrots and onion in the butter until tender. Blend in ¼ cup flour; add the broth. Cook and stir until thickened. Stir in the chicken, mushrooms, wine, celery salt, and Worcestershire sauce. Heat through.

Freeze in a 1-gallon freezer container, with the cheese in a 1-quart freezer bag taped to the side.

To serve, thaw the soup and cheese. Heat the soup. Add the milk and cheese, and heat well; do not boil.

SUMMARY OF PROCESSES: Debone and shred 1 cup rotisserie chicken; shred 1 cup carrots; chop ¼ cup onions.

SERVES 4

FREEZE IN: 1-gallon freezer container; 1-quart Ziploc freezer bag

Melt-in-Your-Mouth Chicken Pie

3 cups deboned and shredded
   rotisserie chicken
1 16-ounce bag frozen mixed
   vegetables
1 cup all-purpose flour
½ teaspoon soda
2 teaspoons baking powder

4 tablespoons butter
1 teaspoon salt
½ teaspoon pepper
1 cup buttermilk
1 10.5-ounce can undiluted cream
   of chicken soup★
2 cups chicken broth★

Combine the chicken and mixed vegetables (still frozen but broken up) in a 1-gallon freezer bag. In a sandwich bag, package the flour, soda, and baking powder. In another sandwich bag package the butter, salt, pepper, and buttermilk. Place the sandwich bags in the gallon bag, label, and freeze. Store marked cans of chicken soup and broth for serving day.

To serve, thaw the ingredients and preheat the oven to 425°F. Spread chicken and vegetables in the bottom of a 13×9×2-inch baking dish treated with nonstick cooking spray. In a bowl combine the cream of chicken soup and chicken broth and spread over the top. Heat butter and buttermilk to melt the butter. Stir in the flour mixture. Spoon this batter on top. Bake, uncovered, 25 to 30 minutes.

SUMMARY OF PROCESSES: Debone and shred 3 cups rotisserie chicken.

SERVES 6

FREEZE IN: 1-gallon Ziploc freezer bag; 2 Ziploc sandwich bags

Mexican Two-Bean Chicken Chili

3 cups deboned and shredded
   rotisserie chicken
1 cup chopped zucchini
1 15-ounce can black beans,
   drained
1 15-ounce can pinto beans,
   drained
1 8.75-ounce can whole kernel corn
4 cups chicken broth

1 14.5-ounce jar thick and chunky
   mild salsa
1 8-ounce can tomato sauce
½ teaspoon chopped garlic
1½ teaspoon chili powder
1 teaspoon ground cumin
1 cup sour cream *
3 chopped plum tomatoes *
Tortilla chips *

Combine all the ingredients, except the sour cream, tomatoes, and tortilla chips in 16-cup freezer container, label, and freeze.

To serve, thaw the chili and place in a slow cooker and cook on low for 7 to 8 hours. Serve with sour cream, chopped tomatoes, and tortilla chips.

SUMMARY OF PROCESSES: Debone and shred 3 cups rotisserie chicken; chop 1 cup zucchini.

SERVES 8

FREEZE IN: 16-cup freezer container

Jerk Chicken and Jerk Pork

1 tablespoon ground allspice
1 tablespoon thyme
1½ teaspoons cayenne pepper
1½ teaspoons pepper
1½ teaspoons ground sage
¾ teaspoon grounds nutmeg
¾ teaspoon grounds cinnamon
2 teaspoons salt
2 teaspoons garlic powder
1 tablespoon sugar
¼ cup soy sauce

¾ cup white vinegar
½ cup orange juice
¼ cup lime juice
¼ cup olive oil
1 Scotch bonnet pepper, or for less
   fire, substitute 1 green bell pepper
½ onion, sliced
⅓ cup chopped green onions
4 boneless, skinless chicken breast
   halves
4 boneless pork loin chops

Pour all the ingredients except the chicken and pork into a blender and puree. Freeze in two batches: place the chicken breasts and half the marinade in a 1-gallon freezer bag, and with the pork loin chops and the remaining of half of the marinade in the other freezer bag.

To serve: thaw and grill or broil the chicken or the pork loin.

SUMMARY OF PROCESSES: Cut ½ onion into slices; chop ⅓ cup green onions, chop 1 Scotch bonnet pepper or 1 green bell pepper.

SERVES 4 for Jerk Chicken; 4 for Jerk Pork

FREEZE IN: 2 1-gallon Ziploc freezer bags

Italian Sausage Soup with Tortellini

1 pound Italian sausage
1 cup chopped onions
1 teaspoon chopped garlic
1 48-ounce carton (6 cups) beef
  broth
½ cup water
½ cup dry red wine or water
1 14.5-ounce can diced tomatoes
1 cup chopped carrots

½ teaspoon dried basil leaves
½ teaspoon dried oregano leaves
1 8-ounce can tomato sauce
1½ cups chopped zucchini
3 tablespoons chopped fresh parsley
½ cup chopped green bell pepper
16 ounces frozen meat- or
  cheese-filled tortellini*
Parmesan cheese*

If sausage comes in casing, remove the casing. Brown the sausage in large pot. Remove the sausage, leaving 1 tablespoon of the drippings in the pot. Sauté the onions and garlic in the reserved drippings until the onions are tender. Add the beef broth, water, wine, tomatoes, carrots, basil, oregano, tomato sauce, cooked sausage, zucchini, parsley, and green bell pepper. Bring to a boil. Reduce the heat and simmer, uncovered, for 30 minutes.

Label and freeze in a 12-cup plastic freezer container with the packages of frozen tortellini attached.

To serve, thaw the soup. Bring to a boil, and then reduce the heat. Add the frozen tortellini and simmer, covered, for 10 minutes, or until the tortellini are tender. Sprinkle Parmesan cheese on top of each serving.

SUMMARY OF PROCESSES: Chop 1 cup onions; chop 1 cup carrots; chop 1½ cups zucchini; chop 3 tablespoons parsley; chop ½ cup green bell peppers.

SERVES 8

FREEZE IN: 12-cup plastic freezer container

Ham with Pineapple Sauce

1 cup brown sugar	1 20-ounce can crushed pineapple,
3 tablespoons apple cider vinegar	including juice
1 tablespoon cornstarch	1¾-pound ham steak

Mix all of the ingredients, except the ham, in a small saucepan. Cook until boiling. Cool and freeze in a 1-quart bag attached to the ham in its packaging.

To serve, thaw and heat the ham in an oven or microwave. Heat the pineapple sauce and pour over ham.

SERVES 6

FREEZE IN: 1-quart Ziploc freezer bag and ham packaging

Chalupa

1 pound (2 cups) dry pinto beans*
½ cup chopped onion
1 4-ounce can chopped green chiles
1 teaspoon chopped garlic
1½ tablespoons chili powder
1½ teaspoons ground cumin
1 teaspoon dried oregano
1 teaspoon salt
2½ cups (10 ounces) shredded mozzarella cheese
3-pound boneless pork loin roast

Store the beans in the pantry. Pour the remaining ingredients, except the cheese, in a 1-gallon freezer bag. Pour the cheese into a sandwich bag. Label the bags, attach them, and freeze.

To serve, thaw and rinse dry beans. Drain and pour the beans into bottom of a slow cooker. Put the pork loin on top, and the remaining ingredients, except for the cheese. Add 3 cups water. Cook on high for 6 hours, or until the meat pulls apart easily and the beans have softened.

Shred the meat. Return it to the slow cooker and cook another 30 to 60 minutes.

Serve in bowls with cheese sprinkled on top.

SUMMARY OF PROCESSES: Chop ½ cup onions.

SERVES 8

FREEZE IN: 1-gallon Ziploc freezer bag; 1 Ziploc sandwich bag

Country-Style Ribs

Salt and pepper to taste
4½ pounds country-style pork loin
ribs
2 cups chopped onion
2 cups chopped green bell peppers

½ cup chopped celery
1 cup red wine
1 28-ounce can diced tomatoes
1 8-ounce can tomato sauce
2 cups beef broth

Salt and pepper meat and place in a 1-gallon freezer bag.

Combine all the other ingredients and pour into another 1-gallon bag. Label and freeze, with the two bags taped together.

To serve, thaw the ribs and place into a slow cooker with the remaining ingredients. Cook on low for 8 to 10 hours—the whole house will smell wonderful.

SUMMARY OF PROCESSES: Chop 2 cups onions, 2 cups green bell peppers, ½ cup celery

SERVES 8

FREEZE IN: 2 1-gallon Ziploc freezer bags

Apricot-Glazed Pork Roast

2 cups chicken broth
1 cup (8 ounces) apricot preserves
2 cups chopped onion

2 tablespoons Dijon mustard
2 tablespoons soy sauce
3½ pounds boneless pork loin roast

Mix the broth, preserves, onion, mustard, and soy sauce. Pour over the pork loin in a 1-gallon freezer bag, label, and freeze. To serve, thaw the pork and cook in a slow cooker on low for 6 to 8 hours.

SUMMARY OF PROCESSES: Chop 2 cups onions.

SERVES 8

FREEZE IN: 1-gallon Ziploc freezer bag

Egg Bake

½ cup chopped onions
2 tablespoons butter
1 12-ounce bag frozen country-style
   hash browns
1 10-ounce package Lit'l Smokies,
   cut into half-inch slices

1½ cups (6 ounces) shredded mild
   cheddar cheese
12 beaten eggs
½ cup milk

Treat a 13×9×2-inch baking dish with nonstick cooking spray. In a skillet, sauté the onions in the butter then place in the prepared baking dish. Spread a layer of frozen hash browns in the bottom of the dish, sprinkle with a layer of meat, then a layer of cheese. In a mixing bowl, beat the eggs briefly, then add the milk. Pour over the cheese layer. Cover with heavy-duty aluminum foil, and freeze.

To serve, thaw and bake in a preheated 375°F oven for 30 to 40 minutes, uncovered. Let sit 5 minutes before cutting into squares.

SUMMARY OF PROCESSES: Chop ½ cup onions; cut Lit'l Smokies in ½-inch slices.

SERVES 8

FREEZE IN: 13×9×2–inch baking dish; heavy-duty aluminum foil

Pork Loin with Sour Cherries

Salt and pepper
4 thick pork loin chops
1 15-ounce can sour cherries

1 tablespoon sugar
Grated zest of ½ lemon
Pinch of ground cinnamon

Season the pork chops with salt and pepper and brown on both sides in their own fat. Place the browned pork chops in the bottom of an 8×8×2-inch baking dish and pour the cherries and their juices over them. Sprinkle sugar, lemon zest, and cinnamon on top. Cover with heavy-duty aluminum foil, label, and freeze.

To serve, thaw the pork chops. Bake, covered, in a preheated 350°F oven for 45 minutes.

SUMMARY OF PROCESSES: Grate zest of ½ lemon

SERVES 4

FREEZE IN: 8×8×2-inch baking dish; heavy-duty aluminum foil

Mediterranean Fish Stew with Spicy Hot Mayonnaise

2 cups chopped onion
1 cup chopped green bell
   pepper
1 teaspoon chopped garlic
2 tablespoons olive oil
½ cup white wine
1 8-ounce bottle clam juice
2 cups chicken broth
1 28-ounce can diced
   tomatoes
¼ teaspoon dried basil
¼ teaspoon dried oregano
¼ teaspoon dried thyme
1½ to 2 pounds cod, frozen

Spicy Mayonnaise:
1 teaspoon chopped garlic
1 teaspoon cayenne pepper
1 tablespoon white wine
   vinegar
¼ teaspoon salt
⅔ cup mayonnaise*
3 red potatoes*
Salt and pepper to taste*

In a large saucepan, sauté the onion, green bell pepper, and chopped garlic in the olive oil. Add remaining ingredients through thyme. Simmer, covered, 10 minutes.

While this is simmering, combine the Spicy Mayonnaise seasoning ingredients in a sandwich bag. Cool the stew and freeze in labeled 1-gallon freezer bag. Attach to it the frozen cod in another 1-gallon freezer bag, and the sandwich bag with the Spicy Mayonnaise. Mark and store the red potatoes in the pantry, and the mayonnaise in the refrigerator.

To serve, thaw the ingredients. Pour the stew into a large pot. Cube the 3 red potatoes and add to the stew. Bring to a boil, reduce the heat, and cook over medium heat for 20 minutes, or until potatoes begin to soften. Cut the thawed cod into 1-inch cubes and add to the stew. Cook another 6 minutes.

Stir the mayonnaise into the Spicy Mayonnaise mixture. Serve the stew with salt and pepper and a dollop of the Spicy Mayonnaise.

SUMMARY OF PROCESSES: Chop 2 cups onion; chop 1 cup green bell pepper.

SERVES 4 to 6

FREEZE IN: 2 1-gallon Ziploc freezer bags; 1 Ziploc sandwich bag

Meat Loaf

2 pounds lean ground beef
¼ teaspoon chili powder
½ cup ketchup
2 eggs
1 cup milk
1 teaspoon dry mustard
1 teaspoon salt
½ cup chopped onion
Pepper to taste
1 teaspoon Worcestershire
   sauce
½ cup dry breadcrumbs
½ cup quick-cooking oatmeal

Sauce:
½ cup ketchup
½ cup packed brown sugar
1 teaspoon mustard

Mix all meat loaf ingredients together and press into a 5×9-inch Pyrex loaf pan. Mix the sauce ingredients and pour into a sandwich bag. Place sauce bag on top of the meat loaf. Cover the loaf pan with heavy-duty aluminum foil, label and freeze.

To serve, thaw the meatloaf. Remove the sauce bag and reserve. Bake the meat loaf in a preheated 350°F oven for 1 hour. Stir the sauce ingredients and spread over the meat loaf; then bake an additional 10 to 15 minutes, or until the meat loaf is no longer pink in center.

SUMMARY OF PROCESSES: Chop ½ cup onion.

SERVES 6

FREEZE IN: 1 5×9-inch Pyrex loaf pan; 1 Ziploc sandwich bag; heavy-duty aluminum foil.

Fajitas

1½ pounds round steak
½ cup lime juice
½ teaspoon chopped garlic
1 teaspoon salt
½ teaspoon pepper
1 green bell pepper

1 red bell pepper
1 onion
2 tablespoons olive oil★
4 large flour tortillas★
½ cup sour cream★
Salsa★

Slice the meat in thin strips and put in a 1-gallon freezer bag with the lime juice, garlic, salt, and pepper. Cut the bell peppers and onion into long strips and place in a 1-quart freezer bag. Tape the two bags together.

To serve, thaw the two bags. Sauté the meat and vegetables in olive oil. Serve wrapped in warmed flour tortillas with sour cream and salsa.

SUMMARY OF PROCESSES: Slice the round steak into thin strips; cut red and green bell peppers and onion into long strips.

SERVES 4

FREEZE IN: 1-gallon Ziploc freezer bag; 1-quart Ziploc freezer bag

Pita Sandwiches

1 pound lean ground beef
1 teaspoon chopped garlic
½ teaspoon paprika
1 teaspoon ground cumin
1 teaspoon ground allspice
¼ teaspoon salt
¼ teaspoon cayenne pepper
6 pita breads, opened and lightly
   grilled★
3 sliced plum tomatoes★
1 small sliced cucumber★

Yogurt Sauce★:
1 6-ounce carton plain yogurt★
1 tablespoon chopped fresh parsley★
2 teaspoons chopped fresh cilantro★
   (optional, not on shopping list)
½ teaspoon dried mint★
Salt and ground pepper to taste★

In a medium skillet, sauté the ground beef. Drain the excess fat, and add the remaining ingredients through the cayenne. Pour into a labeled 1-quart freezer bag and freeze. Mark the pita bread, tomatoes, cucumber, and Yogurt Sauce ingredients and store.

To serve, thaw and warm the filling. Open the end of the pitas to form a sandwich pocket and lightly grill, if desired. Prepare the Yogurt Sauce. Serve the filling on the pita pockets with the yogurt sauce, diced tomatoes, and sliced cucumbers.

SERVES 6

FREEZE IN: 1 quart Ziploc freezer bag

Fiesta Dinner

1 pound lean ground beef
½ cup chopped onion
½ cup chopped celery
½ cup chopped green bell pepper
1 8-ounce can tomato sauce
2 cups beef broth
1 teaspoon sugar
1 teaspoon salt

⅛ teaspoon pepper
½ teaspoon chopped garlic
½ cup uncooked long-grain rice★
4 ounces (½ cup) frozen peas★
1 6-ounce container plain
  yogurt★
1 teaspoon cornstarch★
Chopped fresh parsley for garnish★

Sauté the ground beef in a large skillet over medium-high heat for about 3 minutes. Add the onion, celery, and bell pepper. Continue cooking until the meat is browned. Drain excess fat. Add the tomato sauce, broth, sugar, salt, pepper, and garlic. Pour into a 1-gallon freezer bag, label, and freeze.

To serve, cook the rice according to package directions. Thaw the meat mixture, bring to a boil, cover, and simmer for 8 minutes. Stir in the cooked rice and the peas. Cover and heat 3 to 5 minutes. Remove from heat.

In a small bowl, blend the yogurt and cornstarch until smooth and creamy. Gradually add the yogurt mixture to the meat mixture. Sprinkle with the parsley. Serve immediately.

SUMMARY OF PROCESSES: Chop ½ cup onion; chop ½ cup celery; chop ½ cup green bell pepper.

SERVES 5

FREEZE IN: 1-gallon Ziploc freezer bag

Hot Open-Faced Sandwiches

1 pound lean ground beef
2 cups (8 ounces) shredded
   Colby-Jack cheese
1 2¼-ounce can chopped ripe olives
4 chopped peperoncini peppers

1½ cups chopped onion
½ teaspoon chopped garlic
1 15-ounce can tomato sauce

8 whole-wheat hamburger buns★

In medium skillet, brown the ground beef. Drain excess fat. Add the remaining ingredients, except for the buns. Cook for 10 minutes and pour into a 1-gallon freezer bag. Put the buns into a 1-gallon freezer bag, label, and freeze.

To serve, thaw the mixture and the buns. Place opened buns on cookie sheet and spoon meat mixture evenly on top. Bake in preheated oven at 350-degrees until melted and bubbly.

SUMMARY OF PROCESSES: Chop 1½ cups onions; chop 4 peperoncini peppers

SERVES 8

FREEZE IN: 2 1-gallon Ziploc freezer bags

South-of-the-Border Ground Beef and Corn Pie

1 pound lean ground beef
¼ cup dry breadcrumbs
¼ cup ketchup
2 tablespoon chopped onion
½ teaspoon chopped garlic
½ teaspoon salt
2 teaspoons chili powder
1 teaspoon ground cumin
⅛ teaspoon pepper
2 eggs

¼ cup milk
Dash Tabasco sauce
16 ounces (2 cups) frozen corn
  kernels
⅓ cup chopped green bell pepper
½ cup (2 ounces) shredded mild
  cheddar cheese
½ cup Parmesan cheese
1 2¼-ounce can sliced ripe olives★

Brown the ground beef. Add the next 8 ingredients. Place the mixture in a 1-gallon freezer bag.

Slightly beat the 2 eggs and add the milk and Tabasco. To the egg mixture, add the frozen corn and bell pepper. Place the egg-corn mixture in a 1-quart freezer bag. Package the cheeses in a sandwich bag. Place the smaller bags in the gallon bag, label, and freeze.

To serve, thaw all 3 bags. Spread the meat mixture in a 9-inch pie pan that has been treated with nonstick cooking spray. Put the corn mixture inside the meat "crust." Bake, uncovered, in preheated 375°F oven for 35 to 40 minutes, or until set. Remove from the oven, sprinkle with the two cheeses over the top, and return to the oven for 5 more minutes, or until the cheese is bubbly. Garnish with the ripe olives.

SUMMARY OF PROCESSES: Chop 2 tablespoons onions; chop ⅓ cup green bell peppers.

SERVES 6

FREEZE IN: 1-gallon Ziploc bag; 1-quart Ziploc freezer bag; 1 Ziploc sandwich bag

Barleyburger Stew

1 pound lean ground beef
1 cup chopped onion
½ cup chopped celery
½ cup chopped carrots
5¾ cups (46-ounces) tomato juice

1 teaspoon salt
1½ teaspoons chili powder
1 teaspoon fennel seed
½ teaspoon pepper
½ cup uncooked barley

In medium skillet, sauté the meat, onion, and celery until the meat is browned and the vegetables are translucent. Drain off excess fat. Stir in the remaining ingredients, pour into labeled 1-gallon freezer bag, and freeze.

To serve, thaw the stew. Bring to a boil on the stove reduce the heat, and simmer for 30 minutes. Or cook in a slow cooker on low for 3 hours.

SUMMARY OF PROCESSES: Chop 1 cup onion; chop ½ cup celery; chop ½ cup carrots.

SERVES 6

FREEZE IN: 1-gallon Ziploc freezer bag

Oriental Hotdish

1 pound lean ground beef
½ cup chopped onion
2 cups chopped celery
2 tablespoons olive oil
¼ cup soy sauce
1 cup uncooked long-grain
   rice

1 10.5-ounce can cream of chicken
   soup
1 10.5-ounce can cream of
   mushroom soup
1 12-ounce can bean sprouts,
   undrained
2 cups water

In a skillet, sauté the ground beef, onion, and celery in the olive oil. Cool slightly. Combine with the remaining ingredients and pour into a labeled 1-gallon freezer bag. Freeze.

To serve, thaw the ingredients and pour into a 9×9×2–inch baking dish treated with nonstick cooking spray. Bake at 350°F for 1½ hours.

SUMMARY OF PROCESSES: Chop ½ cup onion; chop 2 cups celery.

SERVES 4

FREEZE IN: 1 gallon Ziploc freezer bag

TWO-WEEK CYCLE C

*N*ew to the Once-A-Month Cooking method? This two-week cycle, with a sampling that runs from Southwestern Egg Casserole through Four Seasons Pizza to Coronation Chicken, might be just the one to try!

Menu Chart for Two-Week Cycle C

RECIPE	SERVINGS	MEAT USED	METHOD	NEEDED TO SERVE	SERVE WITH
Southwestern Egg Casserole	10	Meatless (Eggs)	Bake	Salsa	
Four Seasons Pizza	2–4	Pork: prosciutto	Bake		
Macaroni	6	Ham	Bake	Butter	
Upside-Down Fettuccini Bake	6	Italian sausage	Bake		
Coronation Chicken	6	Boneless, skinless chicken breast halves		Mango	
Chicken and Dumplings	6	Rotisserie chicken	Heat	Biscuits	
Chicken Durango	4	Boneless, skinless chicken breast halves	Bake		
Chicken Scampi	8	Boneless, skinless chicken breast halves	Heat	Fettuccini, tomato	
Texas-Style Lasagna	8	Lean ground beef	Bake		
Beef Pot Roast	8	Beef chuck roast	Slow cooker		
Hamburgers Teriyaki	4	Lean ground beef	Pan-fry or grill	Hamburger buns, lettuce, tomato	
George Romney Meatballs	4	Turkey meatballs	Heat	Wide egg noodles	
Vegetable Soup with Meatballs	6	Turkey meatballs	Heat		
Baked Mediterranean Cod	4	Cod fillets	Heat, bake		

Pantry List for Two-Week Cycle C

Herbs and Spices

Basil, dried: ¼ teaspoon

Bay leaf: 1

Caraway seed: ½ teaspoon

Curry powder: 1 teaspoon

Garlic salt: 1 teaspoon

Ginger, ground: ¾ teaspoon

Nutmeg, ground: dash

Oregano, dried: 3¼ teaspoons

Paprika: 1¼ teaspoon

Parsley flakes: 5½ tablespoons

Pepper

Salt

Thyme: 1 teaspoon

Other

Baking powder: 1 teaspoon

Butter: 2 cups (4 sticks)

Breadcrumbs, dry: 1 cup

Nonstick cooking spray

Eggs: 16 (2★)

Flour: 9½ tablespoons

Honey: 1 tablespoon

Lemon juice: ½ cup

Mayonnaise: ⅔ cup

Mustard, Dijon: ¼ cup

Olive oil: 7 tablespoons

Soy sauce: ¼ cup

Sugar: 1 teaspoon

Teriyaki sauce: 3 tablespoons

Vegetable oil: 1 tablespoon

Vinegar, balsamic: 3 tablespoons

Worcestershire sauce: 2 tablespoons

Freezing Supplies

10 1-gallon Ziploc freezer bags

1 1-quart Ziploc freezer bags

3 Ziploc sandwich bags

2 13×9×2–inch baking dishes

1 12–inch pizza pan

Heavy-duty aluminum foil

Wax paper

1 10-inch quiche dish or cake pan

Indelible marking pen

Freezer tape

SHOPPING LIST FOR TWO-WEEK CYCLE C BY CATEGORIES

An asterisk (★) after an item in the shopping list indicates that the item will not be used until the day the entrée is served. When the item is fresh produce, such as a tomato, you may want to delay purchasing it until close to when you'll served the dish. These items are all listed on the handy Menu Chart so you won't forget to purchase them before they're needed. Incorporate these into a weekly grocery shopping list so that you can continue to minimize trips to the store.

Produce

Basil leaves, fresh: 3

Carrots: 5 medium (2½ cups chopped)

Cashews: 1 11-ounce package (¾ cup needed★)

Celery: 8 stalks (2½ cups chopped)

Garlic, chopped: 1 jar (13 cloves needed)

Green onions: 1 bunch (2 onions [¼ cup chopped])

Lettuce: 1 head★

Mango, large: 1 (1 pound)★

Mushrooms, fresh white: 3 mushrooms

Onions: 3 (½ sliced, 2¼ chopped [4½ cups])

Raisins, golden: ⅓ cup

Tomatoes, fresh: 2★ (1 sliced, 1 chopped)

Zucchini: 1 medium (1 cup chopped)

Dairy/Refrigerator

Buttermilk biscuits, refrigerated:
1 12-ounce tube

Cheddar cheese, shredded mild:
1 8-ounce package
cottage cheese, small curd
(1 48-ounce carton)

Monterey Jack cheese shredded:
1 32-ounce package (28 ounces
needed)

Mozzarella cheese, shredded:
1 8-ounce package (6 ounces
needed)

Parmesan cheese, grated: ½ cup★

Pizza dough: 1 13.8-ounce tube
refrigerated

Sour cream: 1 24-ounce carton
(3 cups needed)

Deli

Prosciutto: 3 thin slices

Frozen

Peas, frozen: 1 8-ounce package
(¼ cup needed)

Meats, Poultry, Fish

Beef, chuck roast: 3 pounds

Beef, lean ground: 3 pounds

**Chicken, boneless, skinless breast
halves:** 12

Chicken, roasted (rotisserie): 1

Cod, frozen fillets: 1 pound

Ham: ⅓ pound

Italian sausage, hot, sweet, or mixed: ½ pounds

Turkey meatballs, Italian-style, ready-to-eat: 3 12-ounce

packages (Look in meat counter with ground turkey. If you can't find them, use frozen meatballs.)

Canned Goods

Artichoke hearts, marinated: 1 14-ounce can (3 halves needed)

Beef broth: 1 14.5-ounce can

Beef consommé: 1 10.5-ounce can

Capers: 1 3.5-ounce jar (1 tablespoon needed)

Chicken broth: 1 32-ounce carton

Green chiles, mild, diced: 1 4-ounce can; 1 7-ounce can

Mango chutney: 1 9-ounce jar (1 tablespoon needed)

Mushroom pieces and stems: 1 8-ounce can

Olives, chopped, pitted ripe: 1 2¼-ounce can

Pizza sauce: 1 6-ounce can

Tomatoes, diced: 2 14.5-ounce cans

Tomatoes, Mexican-style stewed: 1 14.5-ounce can

Tomato sauce: 2 15-ounce cans

Tomatoes, stewed: 1 14.5-ounce can

Turkey gravy: 1 12-ounce jar

Salsa: 1 8-ounce jar (1 cup needed)

Bakery

Buns, hamburger: 4★

Tortillas, flour: 12 (5 needed)

Pasta, Rice

Elbow macaroni: 1 8-ounce
package

Fettuccini: 32-ounce package
(24 ounces needed)★

Noodles, wide egg: 1 12-ounce
package (8 ounces needed)★

Seasonings

Taco seasoning packet: 1-ounce
package

Assembly Order for Two-Week Cycle C

Label freezer containers.

Processing

Put 4 boneless, skinless chicken breast halves in large pot. Add enough lightly salted water to just cover the chicken. Bring to a boil, reduce to a simmer, and cook, covered, for 20 minutes, or until the chicken is no longer pink in the center. Drain and cool the chicken and refrigerate until assembling the chicken dishes.

VEGETABLES AND FRUITS

Artichoke hearts: Cut 3 halves in half

Basil leaves: Thinly slice 3

Carrots: Peel and chop 5 medium carrots (2½ cups)

Celery: Chop 8 stalks (2½ cups)

Green Onions: chop 2 onions (¼ cup chopped)

Mushrooms: Clean and thinly slice 3

Onions: Slice ½ onion into strips; chop remaining 2½ onions (4¼ cups chopped)

Zucchini: Chop 1 (1 cup chopped)

OTHER

Tortillas: Slice 5 flour into 1-inch strips

Prosciutto: Tear 3 thin slices into strips

Ham: Dice 1 cup

CHICKEN

Cut the 4 cooked, cooled chicken breast halves into ½-inch strips

Cut 4 raw boneless, skinless chicken breast halves into 1-inch strips

Debone and shred 1 roasted (rotisserie) chicken

Refrigerate chicken after processing until needed to complete dish

Processing is the most time-consuming task. You've accomplished much!
Now start assembling entrées . . .

EGG

Prepare Southwestern Egg Casserole and freeze.

BEEF

Brown meat for Texas-Style Lasagna.

While ground beef is simmering, prepare Beef Pot Roast and freeze.

Prepare Hamburgers Teriyaki and freeze.

Complete Texas-Style Lasagna and freeze.

Prepare George Romney Meatballs.

Prepare Vegetable Soup with Meatballs and freeze.

FISH

Prepare Baked Mediterranean Cod and freeze.

PORK

Boil macaroni for Macaroni, drain and cool.

Brown ½-pound Italian sausage.

While the sausage is browning, prepare Four Seasons Pizza.

While pizza is baking, drain Italian sausage and set aside for the Upside-Down Fettuccini Bake.

Cool the Four Seasons Pizza and freeze.

Complete Macaroni and freeze.

Prepare Upside-Down Fettuccini Bake. Complete Upside-Down Fettuccini, cool, package, and freeze. Proceed with the chicken dishes if you are waiting for this to finish.

Enjoy the sight of entrées accumulating in your freezer. You're almost finished!

CHICKEN

Prepare Coronation Chicken with cooked chicken strips and freeze.

Prepare Chicken and Dumplings and freeze.

Prepare Chicken Durango and freeze.

Prepare Chicken Scampi and freeze.

Celebrate . . . good meals on hand for many nights ahead!

RECIPES FOR TWO-WEEK CYCLE C

Southwestern Egg Casserole

10 eggs
½ cup all-purpose flour
1 teaspoon baking powder
⅛ teaspoon salt
3 cups (12 ounces) shredded
    Monterey Jack cheese

2 cups (16 ounces) small-curd
    cottage cheese
½ cup melted butter
1 7-ounce can chopped mild green
    chiles
1 cup salsa*

In a medium bowl, beat the eggs with wire whisk. In a separate bowl, combine the flour, baking powder, and salt; stir the eggs into the dry ingredients (the batter will be lumpy). Add the cheeses, butter, and chiles. Pour into a 13×9×2-inch baking dish that has been treated with nonstick cooking spray. Cover with heavy-duty aluminum foil, label, and freeze.

To serve, thaw the egg mixture. Bake, uncovered, in preheated 350°F oven for 30 to 40 minutes, or until a knife inserted near the center comes out clean. Let stand 5 minutes before cutting. Garnish with the salsa.

SERVES 10

FREEZE IN: 13×9×2–inch baking dish; heavy-duty aluminum foil

Texas-Style Lasagna

1½ pounds lean ground beef
2 cups (16 ounces) small-curd
  cottage cheese
2 eggs
1 1-ounce package taco seasoning mix
1 14.5- ounce can diced tomatoes,
  undrained

1 15-ounce can tomato sauce
1 4-ounce can chopped green chiles
5 flour tortillas cut into 1-inch
  strips
4 cups (16 ounces) shredded
  Monterey Jack cheese

In a large skillet, brown the meat. Combine the cottage cheese and eggs in a small bowl. Drain the browned meat of excess fat, and add the taco seasoning, tomatoes, tomato sauce, and chiles; mix well. Simmer, uncovered, for 15 minutes.

In a 13×9×2-inch baking dish treated with nonstick cooking spray, layer half of the meat sauce, half of the tortillas, half of the cottage cheese mixture, and half of the Monterey Jack cheese. Repeat the layers. Cover the with heavy-duty aluminum foil, label, and freeze.

To serve, thaw, and bake, uncovered, in preheated 350°F oven for 40 minutes, or until bubbly. Let stand 10 minutes before serving.

SUMMARY OF PROCESSES: Cut 5 tortillas into 1-inch strips.

SERVES 8

FREEZE IN: 13×9×2-inch baking dish; heavy-duty aluminum foil

Beef Pot Roast

3 pounds beef chuck roast
Salt and pepper to taste
1½ teaspoons chopped garlic
3 tablespoons balsamic vinegar

¼ cup soy sauce
2 tablespoons Worcestershire sauce
¼ cup Dijon mustard

Poke holes in the roast and rub it with salt, pepper, and garlic. In a small bowl stir together the balsamic vinegar, soy sauce, Worcestershire sauce, and Dijon mustard. Place the roast in a labeled 1-gallon freezer bag, pour the marinade over it, and freeze.

To serve, thaw the roast. Place the roast in a slow cooker, with the marinade poured over it. Cook on high 4 to 5 hours, or on low 8 to 10 hours.

SERVES 8

FREEZE IN: 1-gallon Ziploc freezer bag

Hamburgers Teriyaki

1½ pounds lean ground beef
3 tablespoons teriyaki sauce
1 tablespoon honey
1 teaspoon salt
¾ teaspoons ground ginger

1 teaspoon chopped garlic
4 hamburger buns, toasted
Lettuce leaves★
1 sliced tomato★

Combine the ground beef, teriyaki sauce, honey, salt, ginger, and garlic. Shape into 4 patties. Wrap each patty in wax paper, then place in a labeled 1-gallon freezer bag. Place the hamburger buns in a second labeled 1-gallon freezer bag. Tape the bags together and freeze.

To serve, thaw the patties and buns. Pan-fry patties in a large skillet over medium-low heat 20 minutes, turning once (or grill). Serve the patties on buns with the lettuce and tomato.

SERVES 4

FREEZE IN: 2 1-gallon Ziploc freezer bags; wax paper

George Romney Meatballs

Sauce:
2 tablespoons butter
2 tablespoons olive oil
1 cup chopped onion
1 8-ounce can mushrooms, pieces
  and stems
1 10.5-ounce can beef consommé
2 cups (16 ounces) sour cream
1½ tablespoons all-purpose flour
1 teaspoon salt
½ teaspoon caraway seed
Dash nutmeg
8 ounces wide egg noodles★

2 12-ounce packages Italian style,
  ready-to-eat, turkey meatballs
  (Look in the meat counter with
  ground turkey. If you can't find
  them, use frozen meatballs.)

Melt the butter and olive oil in a large skillet over medium heat. Add the onion, mushrooms, and meatballs. Stir in the beef consommé and simmer, covered, for 15 minutes.

Meanwhile, mix together the sour cream, flour, salt, caraway seed, and nutmeg. Pour it into a labeled sandwich bag.

Cool the meatballs and pour into a labeled 1-gallon freezer bag. Tape the two bags together and freeze.

To serve, thaw the contents of both bags and simmer, stirring occasionally, until the mixture is warm and the sauce thickens. Cook the noodles according to package directions. Serve the meat balls over the cooked noodles.

SUMMARY OF PROCESSES: Chop 1 cup onions

SERVES 4

FREEZE IN: 1-gallon Ziploc freezer bag; 1 Ziploc sandwich bag

Vegetable Soup with Meatballs

Soup:
1 14.5-ounce can Mexican-style
    stewed tomatoes
1 15-ounce can tomato sauce
1 14.5-ounce can beef broth
1 cup peeled and chopped carrots
½ sliced onion
1 cup chopped celery
1 cup chopped zucchini
1½ tablespoons dried parsley
½ teaspoon dried oregano

1 12-ounce package Italian style
    ready-to-eat turkey meatballs
    (Look in meat counter with
    ground turkey. If you can't find
    them, use frozen meatballs.)

In a medium mixing bowl, combine all the ingredients except the meatballs and pour into a labeled 1-gallon freezer bag. Tape this bag to the meatball package and freeze.

To serve, thaw the ingredients of both bags. Pour the soup ingredients into a large saucepan. Bring to boil, reduce the heat, and simmer 30 minutes. Add the meatballs and simmer for 10 to 15 minutes, stirring occasionally.

SUMMARY OF PROCESSES: Peel and chop 1 cup carrots; slice ½ of an onion; chop 1 cup celery; chop 1 cup zucchini.

SERVES 6

FREEZE IN: 1-gallon Ziploc freezer bag

Baked Mediterranean Cod

1 tablespoon olive oil
2 cups chopped onion
½ teaspoon chopped garlic
1 14.5-ounce can stewed
  tomatoes
1 tablespoon lemon juice
1 tablespoon capers

1 2¼-ounce can chopped, pitted, ripe
  olives
1 teaspoon sugar
¾ teaspoon dried oregano
¼ teaspoon dried basil
1 pound frozen cod fillets
Salt and pepper to taste

In a medium skillet, heat the olive oil over medium–low heat. Add the onions and cook 5 minutes, or until translucent. Add the garlic and cook 30 seconds. Stir in the tomatoes, lemon juice, capers, olives, sugar, oregano, and basil. Pour into a labeled 1-quart freezer bag and freeze attached to the packaged frozen cod.

To serve, thaw the cod and sauce. Rinse the cod fillets and pat dry. Pour the sauce into a small saucepan. Bring to a boil, then reduce the heat, and simmer 8 to 10 minutes, stirring occasionally. Season to taste with salt and pepper.

Arrange the cod fillets in a single layer in an 8×8×2-inch baking dish treated with nonstick cooking spray. Spoon the sauce over the fish, place in a pre-heated 450°F oven, and bake until the fish is opaque in the center, about 15 minutes. Remove from oven and serve immediately.

SUMMARY OF PROCESSES: Chop 2 cups onions.

SERVES 4

FREEZE IN: 1-quart Ziploc freezer bag

Four Seasons Pizza

1 13.8-ounce tube refrigerated pizza
  dough
1 6-ounce can pizza sauce
1 cup (4 ounces) shredded
  mozzarella cheese

3 thin slices prosciutto, torn in strips
3 marinated artichoke heart halves,
  cut in half
3 thinly sliced mushrooms
3 thinly sliced basil leaves

Preheat oven to 425°F. Spread the dough out on a pizza pan and coat with pizza sauce, to within 1-inch of the edge. Sprinkle with ½ cup of the cheese. Top with prosciutto, artichokes, mushrooms, and basil. Sprinkle with the remaining cheese. Bake for 8 minutes. Do not overbake. Cool, then cover with heavy-duty aluminum foil, label, and freeze.

To serve, remove the pizza from freezer. Preheat the oven to 425°F. Bake the pizza for 5 minutes.

SUMMARY OF PROCESSES: Tear 3 slices prosciutto into strips; cut 3 artichoke halves in half; thinly slice 3 mushrooms and 3 basil leaves.

SERVES 2 to 4

FREEZE IN: 12-inch pizza pan; heavy-duty aluminum foil

Macaroni

1 8-ounce package elbow macaroni
2 cups (8 ounces) shredded mild
  cheddar cheese
2 cups (16 ounces) small-curd
  cottage cheese
⅓ pound ham (1 cup diced)
¼ cup chopped onion

1 large egg
1 cup (8 ounces) sour cream
¼ teaspoon salt
¼ teaspoon pepper
1 cup dry breadcrumbs
¼ teaspoon paprika
2 tablespoons butter★

Cook the macaroni according to package directions until al dente. Drain well and cool. In a large bowl, combine all the ingredients except the breadcrumbs, paprika, and butter. Pour into a labeled 1-gallon freezer bag. Mix together the dry breadcrumbs and paprika in a small bowl. Pour the mixture into a sandwich bag. Attach the two bags and freeze. Store the butter, marked, in refrigerator.

To serve, thaw the ingredients. Melt 2 tablespoons butter. Toss the breadcrumb mixture in it. Pour the macaroni into a 11×7×2-inch baking dish treated with nonstick spray, and spread the breadcrumb mixture on top. Bake, uncovered, in a preheated 350°F oven for 40 to 50 minutes, or until the topping is golden.

Garnish, if desired, with sliced cherry tomatoes and chopped fresh parsley (not on shopping list).

SUMMARY OF PROCESSES: Dice 1 cup ham; chop ¼ cup onion

SERVES 6

FREEZE IN: 1-gallon Ziploc freezer bag; 1 Ziploc sandwich bag

Upside-Down Fettuccini Bake

½ pound Italian sausage (hot, sweet, or mixed)
¼ cup chopped onion
8 ounces fettuccini
1 14.5-ounce can diced tomatoes
1 teaspoon dried oregano

½ cup (2 ounces) shredded mozzarella cheese
½ cup grated Parmesan cheese
3 slightly beaten eggs
2 tablespoons melted butter
2 tablespoons parsley flakes
½ teaspoon chopped garlic

Brown the sausage in a medium skillet. Add the onion during last few minutes. Drain off excess fat. Meanwhile cook the fettuccini according to package directions. Add tomatoes and their liquid to the sausage mixture. Add the oregano and bring to a boil. Reduce the heat and simmer, covered, about 20 minutes, stirring occasionally.

Stir in the mozzarella cheese. Sprinkle ¼ cup of the Parmesan cheese over the tomato mixture.

Mix the eggs, ¼ cup Parmesan cheese, butter, parsley and garlic together in a medium bowl. Toss the noodles with the mixture. Spread the noodle mixture in 10-inch quiche dish or cake pan. Pour the sausage mixture on top. Cover with heavy-duty aluminum foil. Label and freeze.

To serve, thaw and bake, uncovered, in a preheated 350°F about 25 minutes, or until bubbly. Cut into wedges and serve.

SERVES 6

FREEZE IN: 10-inch quiche dish or cake pan; heavy-duty aluminum foil

Coronation Chicken

4 boneless, skinless chicken breast
    halves
⅓ cup golden raisins
⅔ cup mayonnaise
1 teaspoon curry powder

1 tablespoon mango chutney
1 teaspoon lemon juice
Salt and pepper to taste
¾ cup toasted cashews
1 (1 pound) large mango★

In a large pot, cook the chicken in lightly salted boiling water for 20 minutes. Drain, cool, and cut into ½-inch strips. In a medium bowl, stir together the chicken strips and raisins. In another medium bowl, mix together the mayonnaise, curry powder, chutney, and lemon juice. Season with salt and pepper, then toss gently with the chicken mixture. Pour into a labeled 1-gallon freezer bag, and pour the cashews into a sandwich bag. Attach the two bags together and freeze. Store the mango in refrigerator.

To serve, thaw the chicken and cashews. Toast the cashews, and peel and slice mango. Stir half the nuts and half the mango slices into the chicken. Garnish with remaining nuts and mango. Serve cold.

SUMMARY OF PROCESSES: Cook 4 boneless, skinless chicken breast halves for 20 minutes, cool, cut into ½-inch strips.

SERVES 6

FREEZE IN: 1-gallon Ziploc freezer bag; 1-Ziploc sandwich bag

Chicken and Dumplings

1 roasted (rotisserie) chicken,
   deboned and shredded
1 tablespoon vegetable oil
1 tablespoon butter
1½ cups chopped carrots
1½ cups chopped celery
1 cup chopped onion
4 cups water

1 32-ounce carton chicken broth
1 teaspoon dried thyme
1 bay leaf
1 12-ounce jar turkey gravy
¼ cup frozen peas (do not defrost)
1 12-ounce tube refrigerated
   buttermilk biscuits*

Mix all the ingredients, except the biscuits, in a large bowl. Pour into a 1-gallon freezer bag, label, and freeze. Mark the tube of biscuits and store in the refrigerator.

To serve, thaw the ingredients in the bag. Place in a saucepan (with a lid), and warm over medium heat until hot and bubbling. While the chicken mixture is heating, unroll the biscuits and cut each into four pieces. Push the biscuit pieces into the hot bubbling liquid with a wooden spoon, a few at a time, until they are all in. Cover and simmer for 10 minutes.

SUMMARY OF PROCESSES: Debone and shred roasted rotisserie chicken; chop 1½ cups carrots; chop 1½ cups celery; chop 1 cup onion

SERVES 6

FREEZE IN: 1-gallon Ziploc freezer bag

Chicken Durango

½ cup melted butter
5 tablespoons lemon juice
1 teaspoon garlic salt
1 teaspoon paprika

1 teaspoon dried oregano
Salt and pepper to taste
4 boneless, skinless chicken breast
halves

Combine all ingredients except the chicken in a small bowl. Put the chicken into a labeled 1-gallon freezer bag, pour other ingredients over it, and freeze.

To serve, thaw the ingredients. Place in a 11×9×2-inch baking dish treated with nonstick cooking spray. Bake, uncovered, at 325°F for 45 minutes.

SERVES 4

FREEZE IN: 1-gallon Ziploc freezer bag

Chicken Scampi

¼ cup chopped green onions
3 teaspoons chopped garlic
½ cup butter
¼ cup olive oil
1 tablespoon lemon juice
4 pounds boneless, skinless chicken
   breast halves, cut into 1-inch
   strips

2 tablespoons dried parsley
½ teaspoon pepper
1 16-ounce package fettuccini★
1 chopped tomato★

In a large skillet, sauté the green onions and garlic in the butter and oil. Add the lemon juice, chicken, parsley, and pepper. Cook the chicken, stirring occasionally, for 12 to 15 minutes, until it is no longer pink inside. Cool. Pour into a labeled 1-gallon freezer bag and freeze.

To serve, thaw the chicken mixture. Cook the fettuccini according to package directions. In a large skillet, cook the chicken mixture over medium heat for 6 to 10 minutes, or until chicken is heated through. Spoon the chicken over fettuccini. Garnish with chopped tomato.

SERVES 8

FREEZE IN: 1-gallon Ziploc freezer bag

TWO-WEEK CYCLE D

*F*eeding a hungry sports team or having a sleepover? The Barbecued Chicken for Buns in this cycle, as well as the Meatball Sub Casserole, will handle a hungry crowd.

Menu Chart for Two-Week Cycle D

RECIPE	SERVINGS	MEAT USED	METHOD	NEEDED TO SERVE	SERVE WITH
Meatball Sub Casserole	8	Turkey meatballs	Bake		
Easy Spaghetti Sauce	8	Lean ground beef	Heat	Spaghetti, mozzarella cheese	
Orecchiette with Tuna	6	Tuna	Heat	Orecchiette pasta	
Sweet Mustard Grilled Pork	8	Pork loin	Grill or bake	Cooking spray	
Milanesa	4	Round steak	Bake	Lemon	
Chicken Naranja	4	Boneless, skinless chicken breast halves	Bake	Rice	
Chicken Dijon	4	Boneless, skinless chicken breast halves	Heat	Tomatoes, parsley flakes	
Barbecued Chicken for Buns	16–20	Boneless, skinless chicken breast halves	Slow cooker	Sandwich buns	
Chicken Italiano	8	Boneless, skinless chicken breast halves	Bake	Tomatoes	
Tilapia Fillets	4	Tilapia	Bake	Tomatoes, olive oil	
Mini Cheese Meat Loaves	4	Lean ground beef	Bake		
Gnocchi with Turkey Ragu	8	Ground turkey	Heat	Gnocchi, basil, Parmesan cheese, pepper	
Poppy Seed Chicken	8	Boneless, skinless chicken breast halves	Bake	Butter	
Craig and Debbie's Easy Fixin's	4	Lean ground beef	Heat	Corn chips	

PANTRY LIST FOR TWO-WEEK CYCLE D

Herbs and Spices

Basil, leaves: 2 teaspoons

Bay leaf: 1

Cilantro leaves: 1 teaspoon (optional)

Crushed red pepper: pinch

Cumin: 1½ teaspoons

Dry mustard: 2 teaspoons

Ginger, ground: 1 teaspoon

Italian seasoning: 1 teaspoon

Oregano, dried: 1¼ teaspoons

Parsley flakes: 3 tablespoons

Pepper

Poppy seeds: 2 tablespoons

Salt

Thyme: ½ teaspoon

Other

Brown sugar: ¾ cup

Butter: 1 cup, 1 tablespoon (2⅛ sticks)

Cooking spray

Cornstarch: 2 tablespoons★

Eggs: 3

Flour: 2 tablespoons

Ketchup: 2⅓ cups

Lemon juice: 1 tablespoon

Mayonnaise: ¾ cup

Milk: ¾ cup

Molasses: ½ cup

Mustard, Dijon: 6 tablespoons

Mustard, prepared: 1½ teaspoons

Oatmeal, quick-cooking: ½ cup

Olive oil: 4 tablespoons

Orange juice: 1 cup

Soy sauce: ½ cup

Vinegar, red wine: 2 tablespoons

Vinegar, white: 6 tablespoons

Wine, white, dry: ½ cup

Freezing Supplies

13 1-gallon Ziploc freezer bags

4 1-quart Ziploc freezer bags

5 Ziploc sandwich bags

Heavy-duty aluminum foil

1 8×8×2-inch baking dish

1 13×9×2-inch baking dish

Indelible marking pen

Freezer tape

SHOPPING LIST FOR TWO-WEEK CYCLE D BY CATEGORIES

An asterisk (★) after an item in the shopping list indicates that the item will not be used until the day the entrée is served. When the item is fresh produce, such as a tomato, you may want to delay purchasing it until close to when you'll served the dish. These items are all listed on the handy Menu Chart so you won't forget to purchase them before they're needed. Incorporate these into a weekly grocery shopping list so that you can continue to minimize trips to the store.

Produce

Basil leaves fresh: 1 bunch (1 cup chopped)

Celery: 6 medium stalks (3 cups chopped)

Garlic, chopped: 1 jar (11 cloves needed)

Green bell pepper: 2 (2⅓ cups chopped)

Lemons: 2

Onions: 2 (4 cups chopped)

Onions, red: 1 (2 cups chopped)

Red bell pepper: 1 (½ cup chopped)

Tomatoes: 6★

Tomatoes, grape: 1 pint

Dairy

Mozzarella cheese, shredded: 1 24-ounce package (20 ounces needed)★

Cheddar cheese, sharp, shredded: 1 8-ounce package (4 ounces needed)

Cream cheese: 2 8-ounce packages

Half-and-half: ½ pint (½ cup
   needed)

Parmesan cheese; grated: 2½ cups

Sour cream: 1 8-ounce carton
   (1 cup needed)

Frozen

Corn, frozen: 1 16-ounce bag
   (need 1½ cups)

Spinach, chopped, frozen:
   1 16-ounce bag

Meats, Poultry, Fish

Beef, lean ground: 4 pounds

Beef, round steak: 1 pound

Chicken, boneless, skinless breast
   halves: 24

Pork loin roast: 3 pounds

Tilapia fillets, frozen: 4

Turkey, ground: 2 pounds

Turkey meatballs, Italian-style,
   ready-to-eat: 2 12-ounce
   packages (in meat counter
   with ground turkey)

Canned Goods

Black beans: 1 15-ounce can

Chicken broth: 1 14.5-ounce can
   (1 cup needed)

Mushroom pieces and stems:
   1 4-ounce can

Olives, sliced ripe pitted:
   1 2¼-ounce can

Pimientos: 1 2-ounce jar

Salsa—mild, medium or hot:
   1 16-ounce jar (⅔ cup needed)

Cream of celery soup:
   1 10.5-ounce can

Cream of chicken soup:
   1 10.5-ounce can

Tomato soup: 3 26-ounce cans

Tomato paste: 1 6-ounce can

Tomato sauce: 1 15-ounce can

Tuna, oil packed: 2 6-ounce cans

V8 juice: 2 5.5-ounce cans

Bakery

Buns, sandwich: 24★

Italian bread: 1 loaf

Pasta, Rice

Gnocchi: 1 16-ounce box★ (potato dumplings, look on pasta aisle or with frozen pasta)

Orecchiette (or other small shell pasta): 1 16-ounce package

Rice: 1 cup uncooked★

Uncle Ben's Original Long-Grain and Wild Rice: 1 6-ounce box

Spaghetti: 1 16-ounce package★

Other

Corn chips: 1 9.5-ounce bag

Italian-seasoned breadcrumbs: (1½ cups needed)

Ritz crackers: 1 sleeve (35 crackers)

ASSEMBLY ORDER FOR TWO-WEEK CYCLE D

Label freezer containers.

Processing

VEGETABLES AND FRUITS

Cilantro: Chop 1 tablespoon (optional)

Celery: Chop 6 stalks (3 cups)

Green bell pepper: Chop 2 (2⅓ cups)

Lemon: 1 (Grate 4 teaspoons zest; squeeze 4 teaspoons juice)

Onions: Chop 2 (4 cups chopped)

Red bell pepper: Chop ½ (½ cup)

Red onion: chop 1 (2 cups chopped)

Spinach, frozen: Thaw, drain and squeeze dry

Tomatoes, grape: Halve one pint

BREAD/RICE

Cube Italian bread loaf into 6 cups of small pieces.

Crush 1 sleeve Ritz crackers (35 crackers).

Cook box of Uncle Ben's Rice according to package directions.

POULTRY

Cube 6 chicken breast halves for Barbecued Chicken for Buns.

Refrigerate until needed.

Cut 4 chicken breast halves into strips for Chicken Naranja and 6 chicken breast halves into strips for Poppy Seed Chicken. Refrigerate until needed (divide into two bags to remember they're for two recipes).

Cut 8 chicken breast halves in half for Chicken Dijon and Chicken Italiano. Refrigerate until needed (divide into two bags to remember they're for two recipes).

BEEF

Pound round steak until very thin. Refrigerate until needed.

Processing is the most time-consuming task. You've accomplished much! Now start assembling entrées . . .

FISH

Prepare Tilapia Fillets and freeze.

Prepare Orecchiette with Tuna and freeze.

PORK

Prepare Sweet Mustard Grilled Pork and freeze.

POULTRY

Cook 6 chicken breast strips in water with spices for Poppy Seed Chicken.

Brown chicken breasts for Chicken Dijon.

Prepare Barbecued Chicken for Buns and freeze.

Finish Poppy Seed Chicken and freeze.

Finish Chicken Dijon and freeze.

Prepare Chicken Naranja and freeze.

Prepare Chicken Italiano and freeze.

Prepare Gnocchi and Turkey Ragu and freeze.

Congratulate yourself for the time and money you are saving on meals this month! You're almost finished!

BEEF

Prepare Easy Spaghetti Sauce. Set aside 2 cups of the sauce to use for Meatball Sub Casserole and freeze the remaining sauce for Spaghetti.

Prepare Meatball Sub Casserole and freeze.

Brown ground beef for Craig and Debbie's Easy Fixin's.

Prepare Mini Cheese Meat Loaves and freeze.

Complete Craig and Debbie's Easy Fixin's and freeze.

Prepare Milanesa and freeze.

Celebrate . . . You did it!

RECIPES FOR TWO-WEEK CYCLE D

Tilapia Fillets

4 frozen tilapia fillets
1 2¼-ounce can olives, sliced, pitted
   ripe drained
¼ cup grated Parmesan cheese

1 lemon (4 teaspoons zest and
   4 teaspoons juice)
¼ cup mayonnaise
2 tomatoes★
1 tablespoon olive oil★

Leave the tilapia fillets frozen until serving day. Combine remaining ingredients, except for the tomatoes and olive oil, in a small bowl, then pour into a sandwich bag, and slip this bag into a labeled 1-gallon freezer bag with the frozen tilapia fillets (still in their store packaging). Freeze.

To serve, thaw the fish and sauce. Preheat the oven to 325°F. Rinse and blot the fish dry with paper towels. Line prepared 9×9×2-inch baking dish that has been treated with nonstick cooking spray, with sliced fresh tomatoes. Place the fillets on top of the tomatoes. Sprinkle with olive oil. Spread with the Parmesan cheese mixture. Bake 20 minutes.

SUMMARY OF PROCESSES: Grate 4 teaspoons lemon zest; squeeze 4 teaspoons lemon juice.

SERVES 4

FREEZE IN: 1-gallon Ziploc freezer bag; 1 Ziploc sandwich bag and tilapia packaging

Orecchiette with Tuna

Pinch crushed red pepper flakes
1 teaspoon chopped garlic
1 tablespoon olive oil
2 5.5-ounce cans V8 juice
1 pint halved grape tomatoes
2 6-ounce cans drained light tuna
 in oil

1 tablespoon lemon juice
2 tablespoons melted
 butter
1 tablespoon basil leaves
1 16-ounce package orecchiette
 (or small elbow) pasta★

In a skillet, sauté the crushed red pepper and garlic in the oil for 1 minute. Add the V8 juice, increase the heat to high, and bring the mixture to a boil.

Reduce the heat to low, add grape tomatoes, and cook 4 minutes. Stir in the tuna, lemon juice, butter, and basil leaves. Pour into a labeled 1-quart freezer bag and freeze. Store marked package of pasta in the pantry.

To serve, thaw the ingredients. Cook the pasta according to package directions. Warm the sauce and toss gently with the pasta.

SUMMARY OF PROCESSES: Cut pint of grape tomatoes in half; chop ½ cup fresh basil.

SERVES 6

FREEZE IN: 1-quart Ziploc freezer bag

Sweet Mustard Grilled Pork

½ cup molasses
¼ cup Dijon mustard
2 tablespoons white vinegar

1 teaspoon salt
3 pounds pork loin roast
Cooking spray★

Combine the first four ingredients; brush half of mixture over the pork loin. Put the pork loin into a labeled 1-gallon freezer bag. Pour the remaining marinade in a sandwich bag and slip the small bag inside the larger one. Freeze.

To serve, thaw the ingredients. Coat a grill rack with cooking spray. Place the pork loin on grill over medium-hot coals (350 to 400°F). Cover with grill lid and cook 25 to 30 minutes, or until a thermometer inserted into thickest portion registers 160°F, turning once and basting with reserved molasses glaze during the last 8 minutes. If you would rather, place the roast on a rack in a shallow roasting pan and roast in a 325°F oven for 2 hours, or until a meat thermometer registers 160°F.

SERVES 8

FREEZE IN: 1-gallon Ziploc freezer bag; 1 Ziploc sandwich bag

Poppy Seed Chicken

6 boneless, skinless chicken breast
    halves, cut into strips
½ teaspoon dried thyme
1 teaspoon salt
¼ teaspoon pepper
1 bay leaf
1 10.5-ounce can cream of celery
    soup
1 10.5-ounce can chicken soup

1 cup (8 ounces) sour cream
1 6-ounce package Original Uncle
    Ben's Long-Grain and Wild Rice
½ cup chicken broth (from boiled
    chicken)
1 sleeve Ritz crackers, crushed
    (35 crackers)
2 tablespoons poppy seeds
½ cup (1 stick) butter*

Cook the chicken breasts in a quart of water with the thyme, salt, pepper, and bay leaf. Meanwhile prepare the rice. When the chicken is done, about 20 minutes, reserve ½ cup chicken broth, and cool the cooked chicken.

Mix the cooled chicken with the remaining ingredients, including the reserved ½ cup chicken broth. Pour into a labeled 1-gallon freezer bag and freeze. Store the Ritz cracker crumbs and poppy seeds in bag attached. Mark and store the stick of butter.

To serve, thaw the chicken mixture. Pour into 13×9 2-inch baking dish treated with nonstick cooking spray. Melt the butter. Mix the topping of melted butter and crushed Ritz crackers and poppy seeds, and sprinkle on top of the chicken mixture. Bake in preheated 350°F oven for 30 minutes.

SUMMARY OF PROCESSES: Cook 6 boneless, skinless chicken breast halves in water with spices; cook Uncle Ben's Rice according to package directions; crush 1 sleeve of Ritz crackers.

SERVES 8

FREEZE IN: 1-gallon Ziploc freezer bag; 1 Ziploc sandwich bag

Chicken Dijon

3 tablespoons butter
4 boneless, skinless chicken breast
halves, cut in half
2 tablespoons all-purpose flour
1 cup chicken broth

½ cup half-and-half
2 tablespoons Dijon mustard
2 tomatoes, cut in wedges★
2 tablespoons parsley flakes★

Melt the butter in a large skillet. Cook the chicken breast pieces in the butter over medium heat until cooked through and lightly browned, about 20 minutes. Remove the chicken from the skillet and set aside to cool.

Stir flour into drippings in the skillet and cook for 1 minute. Add the chicken broth and half-and-half. Stir and cook until the sauce thickens and bubbles. Stir in the mustard. Cool the sauce. Pour the chicken and cooled sauce into a labeled 1-gallon freezer bag and freeze.

To serve, thaw the chicken. Place the chicken and sauce in a skillet, cover, and heat for 10 minutes. Garnish with tomatoes and sprinkle with parsley flakes.

SUMMARY OF PROCESSES: Cut 4 boneless, skinless chicken breast halves in half.

SERVES 4

FREEZE IN: 1-gallon Ziploc freezer bag

Barbecued Chicken for Buns

6 cubed boneless, skinless chicken
    breast halves
2 cups chopped celery
1 cup chopped onions
1 cup chopped green bell peppers
4 tablespoons butter
2 cups ketchup

2 cups water
2 tablespoons brown sugar
¼ cup white vinegar
2 teaspoons dry mustard
1 teaspoon pepper
1 teaspoon salt
24 sandwich buns★

In a large bowl, stir together all the ingredients except for the sandwich buns. Pour into a labeled 1-gallon bag and freeze. Slip the buns into 2 more 1-gallon freezer bags and attach to the chicken bag.

To serve, thaw the barbecued chicken and the rolls. Pour the chicken into a slow cooker, cover, and cook on low for 6 to 8 hours. Stir the chicken until it shreds. Pile the shredded chicken into the rolls and serve.

Summary of Processes: Cube 6 boneless, skinless chicken breast halves; chop 2 cups celery; chop 1 cup onions; chop 1 cup green bell pepper.

NOTE: This may be frozen as two or three entrées instead of one large one.

SERVES 16 to 20

FREEZE IN: 3 1-gallon Ziploc freezer bags

Chicken Naranja

4 boneless, skinless chicken breast
  halves, cut into strips
1 teaspoon ground ginger
1 cup chopped celery
1 cup orange juice

½ cup soy sauce
⅓ cup packed brown sugar
2 tablespoons cornstarch
½ cup water
1 cup uncooked rice★

Place the chicken, ginger, and celery in a labeled 1-gallon freezer bag. Mix the orange juice, soy sauce, brown sugar, cornstarch, and water in a Pyrex measuring cup and pour over other ingredients. Freeze.

To serve, thaw the ingredients. Preheat the oven to 350°F. Bake, uncovered, for 60 minutes. Cook the rice according to package directions. Serve the chicken over the cooked rice.

SUMMARY OF PROCESSES: Cut 4 boneless, skinless chicken breast halves into strips; chop 1 cup celery.

SERVES 4

FREEZE IN: 1-gallon Ziploc freezer bag

Chicken Italiano

1 16-ounce bag frozen chopped
   spinach, thawed, drained, and
   squeezed dry
1 8-ounce package cream cheese
4 boneless, skinless chicken breast
   halves, cut in half
½ cup Italian-seasoned
   breadcrumbs

¼ teaspoon dried oregano
1 tablespoon olive oil
1 cup (4 ounces) shredded
   mozzarella cheese
¼ cup grated Parmesan cheese
2 fresh tomatoes*

Combine the spinach and cream cheese in mixer or food processor. Pour into a 1-quart freezer bag.

Dredge the chicken breast halves in the breadcrumbs and oregano.

Heat the olive oil in skillet and cook the chicken for 2 minutes on each side, or until lightly browned. Cool. Put the chicken into a labeled 1-gallon freezer bag. Store the mozzarella and Parmesan cheeses in sandwich bag. Attach to freezer bag. Also attach the bag with the spinach mixture. Store the fresh tomatoes in the pantry.

To serve, thaw the ingredients. Press the spinach mixture in bottom of a 13×9×2-inch baking dish treated with nonstick cooking spray. Arrange the chicken over the top of the spinach mixture. Layer fresh tomato slices on top and sprinkle with the cheeses. Bake in preheated 350°F oven for 30 minutes.

SUMMARY OF PROCESSES: Thaw, drain, and squeeze dry 1 16-ounce package chopped spinach; cut 4 boneless, skinless chicken breast halves in half.

SERVES 8

FREEZE IN: 1-gallon Ziploc freezer bag; 1-quart Ziploc freezer bag; 1 Ziploc sandwich bag

Gnocchi with Turkey Ragu

2 pounds ground turkey
1 tablespoon olive oil
2 cups chopped red onion
1⅓ cups chopped green bell pepper
3 teaspoons chopped garlic
1 tablespoon basil leaves
1 teaspoon salt

½ cup dry white wine
1 6-ounce can tomato paste
1 15-ounce can tomato sauce
2 cups grated Parmesan cheese
1 16-ounce box gnocchi★
Pepper to taste★

In a large skillet, coated with nonstick cooking spray, brown the turkey. Transfer the browned turkey to a bowl. Add olive oil to the skillet. Put the onion, bell pepper, garlic, basil leaves, and salt in the skillet and sauté for 5 minutes. Return the turkey to the skillet and add the wine, stirring lightly. Stir in the tomato paste and tomato sauce. Cool and freeze in a labeled 1-gallon bag. Store the cheese in a 1-quart bag attached. Store the marked package of gnocchi in the pantry.

To serve, thaw the ragu. Cook the gnocchi according to package directions. Warm the ragu. Drain the cooked gnocchi and put in the bottom of shallow bowls. Top with the ragu and sprinkle generously with cheese and pepper.

SUMMARY OF PROCESSES: Chop 2 cups red onion; chop 1⅓ cups green bell pepper.

SERVES 8

FREEZE IN: 1-gallon Ziploc freezer bag; 1 quart Ziploc freezer bag

Easy Spaghetti Sauce

2 pounds lean ground beef
2½ cups chopped onions
1 teaspoon dried oregano
1 teaspoon dried sweet basil
Salt and pepper to taste
3 26-ounce cans tomato soup

1 4-ounce can mushrooms pieces
  and stems
1 2-ounce jar pimientos
2 cups (8 ounces) shredded
  mozzarella cheese★
1 16-ounce package spaghetti★

Brown the ground beef in large pot. Add the onions and sauté until translucent and meat is no longer pink. Add the oregano, basil, salt, and pepper. Add the tomato soup and simmer for 10 minutes. Add the mushrooms and pimientos. Stir, cool, and freeze all but 2 cups in a labeled 1-gallon freezer bag. Reserve the remaining 2 cups sauce for Meatball Sub Casserole (next recipe). Put the mozzarella cheese into a 1-quart freezer bag and attach to the other bag. Mark the spaghetti package and store in the pantry.

To serve, thaw spaghetti sauce. Heat and serve over spaghetti, cooked according to package directions. Top each serving with shredded cheese.

SUMMARY OF PROCESSES: Chop 2½ cups onion.

SERVES 8

FREEZE IN: 1 gallon Ziploc freezer bag; 1 quart Ziploc freezer bag

Meatball Sub Casserole

6 cups cubed Italian bread
1 8-ounce package softened cream
   cheese
½ cup mayonnaise
1 teaspoon Italian seasoning
½ teaspoon pepper
2 cups (8 ounces) shredded
   mozzarella cheese

1 cup water
2 cups Easy Spaghetti Sauce (from
   previous recipe)
2 12-ounce packages turkey
   meatballs, Italian-style,
   ready-to-eat

Spread the bread cubes in a 13×9×2-inch baking dish treated with nonstick cooking spray. Combine the cream cheese, mayonnaise, Italian seasoning, and pepper and pour over the bread. Cover with ½ cup mozzarella cheese.

Combine the water, spaghetti sauce, and meatballs and pour over cheese layer in the baking dish. Top with the remaining cheese. Cover with heavy-duty aluminum foil, label, and freeze.

To serve, thaw the casserole. Bake in preheated 350°F oven for 30 minutes.

SUMMARY OF PROCESSES: Cube Italian bread to make 6 cups.

SERVES 8

FREEZE IN: 13×9×2-inch baking dish; heavy-duty aluminum foil

Craig and Debbie's Easy Fixin's

1 pound lean ground beef
2/3 cup salsa
1 15-ounce can black beans, drained
1 1/2 cups frozen corn

1/2 cup chopped red bell pepper
1 teaspoon cilantro leaves (optional)
1 1/2 teaspoons cumin
1 9.5-ounce bag corn chips*

Brown the ground beef. Cool. Add the other ingredients, except the corn chips, label, and freeze in a 1-gallon bag. Mark the bag of corn chips and store in the pantry.

To serve, thaw the ingredients. Place the fixin's in a saucepan and heat for 7 minutes. Serve with corn chips.

SUMMARY OF PROCESSES: Chop 1/2 cup red bell pepper, chop 1 tablespoon cilantro.

SERVES 4

FREEZE IN: 1-gallon Ziploc freezer bag

Mini Cheese Meat Loaves

1 egg
¾ cup milk
1 cup (4 ounces) shredded cheddar
   cheese
½ cup quick-cooking oats
½ cup chopped onion

1 teaspoon salt
1 pound lean ground beef
⅓ cup ketchup
¼ cup packed brown sugar
1 teaspoon prepared mustard

In large bowl, whisk the egg and milk. Stir in the cheese, oats, onion, and salt. Add the beef and mix well (easiest with your hands). Shape into 2 loaves. Place the loaves into a 8×8×2-inch baking dish treated with nonstick cooking spray. Combine the ketchup, brown sugar, and mustard in a small bowl. Spoon the sauce over the loaves. Cover the baking dish with heavy-duty aluminum foil, label, and freeze.

To serve, thaw the loaves. Bake, uncovered, in a preheated 350°F oven for 45 minutes.

SUMMARY OF PROCESSES: Chop ½ cup onion.

SERVES 4

FREEZE IN: 13×9×2-inch baking dish; heavy-duty aluminum foil

Milanesa

1 pound round steak
2 eggs
2 tablespoons red wine vinegar
1½ teaspoons chopped garlic

1 tablespoon parsley flakes
Salt to taste
1 cup Italian-seasoned breadcrumbs
1 lemon★

Pound the steak until very thin. Whisk together all the ingredients except the breadcrumbs and the lemon and pour into a labeled 1-gallon freezer bag with the steak. Put dry breadcrumbs in a sandwich bag and store the lemon in the refrigerator. Attach the two bags and freeze.

To serve, thaw the steak and discard the marinade. Dredge the steak in the breadcrumbs. Place into a 8×8×2-inch baking dish prepared with nonstick cooking spray and bake at 350°F for about 15 minutes. Serve with lemon slices.

SUMMARY OF PROCESSES: Pound steak until very thin.

SERVES 4

FREEZE IN: 1-gallon Ziploc freezer bag; 1 Ziploc sandwich bag

GLUTEN-FREE TWO-WEEK CYCLE

*T*ired of searching for delicious entrées that are gluten free? These recipes are chosen to be both healthy and tasty for the whole family.

Menu Chart for Gluten-Free Two-Week Cycle

RECIPE	SERVINGS	MEAT USED	METHOD	NEEDED TO SERVE	SERVE WITH
BBQ Roast	8	Beef: London broil	Grill or broil		
Mediterranean Burgers	4	Lean ground beef	Grill	Gluten-free rolls; tomato, cucumber, red onion, romaine leaves	
Old-Fashioned Meat Loaf	6	Lean ground beef	Bake		
Szechwan Chicken and Peanuts	4	Boneless, skinless chicken breasts	Stir-fry	Oil, peanuts, brown rice	
Cashew Chicken	4	Boneless, skinless chicken breasts	Bake	Rice, cashews	
Slow Cooker Artichoke, Chicken, and Olives	6	Boneless, skinless chicken breasts	Slow cooker	Brown rice	
Honey-Ginger Chicken Bites	6	Boneless, skinless chicken breasts	Bake then broil	Sesame seeds	
Chicken à l'Orange	8–12	Boneless, skinless chicken breasts	Bake	Mandarin oranges, brown rice	
Nanner's Chicken Kebabs	4	Boneless, skinless chicken breasts	Grill	Red potatoes, mushrooms, pineapple chunks slices, onion, green bell pepper	
Parsley, Sage, Rosemary, and Thyme Chicken	6	Whole roaster chicken	Bake		
Penne with Chickpeas	4	Meatless	Heat	Gluten-free penne or mostaccioli pasta, gluten-free Parmesan cheese	
Vegan Creamy Tomato Soup	4	Meatless	Heat	Lemon (juice and zest)	
Teriyaki Tuna Steaks	4	Fish: Tuna steaks	Grill		
Swedish Yellow Split Pea Soup	6	Ham shank or ham bone	Heat	Beer, cider vinegar	

PANTRY LIST FOR GLUTEN-FREE TWO-WEEK CYCLE

Herbs and Spices

Cardamon, ground: ¾ teaspoon

Cayenne pepper: dash

Curry powder: 1 tablespoon

Dill weed: 1 tablespoon

Ginger, ground: 4¾ teaspoons

Marjoram: ¼ teaspoon

Oregano: 1 teaspoon

Paprika: 1 teaspoon

Parsley flakes: 2 tablespoons

Pepper

Red pepper flakes, crushed: 1¼ teaspoons

Rosemary, leaves: 2 teaspoons

Sage, ground: 1 teaspoon

Salt

Seasoned salt: 1 teaspoon

Sesame seeds: 2 teaspoons

Tarragon, dried: 1 teaspoon

Thyme, dried: 1¾ teaspoons

Other

Brown sugar: 3 tablespoons

Butter: ½ cup

Chicken bouillon, gluten-free: 1 tablespoon

Cooking spray, gluten-free

Cornstarch: 4 teaspoons★

Eggs: 2

Honey: ⅔ cup

Ketchup: 2 tablespoons

Lemon juice: 6 tablespoons

Mustard, Dijon, gluten-free:
⅓ cup

Oats, old-fashioned, gluten-free:
¾ cup

Oil, olive: 1⅔ cups

Oil, dark sesame: 2 teaspoons

Orange juice: 2 cups

Sherry, dry: ¼ cup

Sugar: 3¼ teaspoons

Tabasco sauce, gluten-free: 2 dashes

Tapioca, quick-cooking:
3 tablespoons

Vegetable oil: ¾ cup

Vinegar, apple cider (if distilled it
is gluten-free): ¼ cup

Vinegar, distilled white:
2 tablespoons

Vinegar, red wine (if distilled it's
gluten-free): ⅓ cup

Wine, white: ½ cup

Freezing Supplies

12 1-gallon Ziploc freezer bags

2 1-quart Ziploc freezer bags

9 Ziploc sandwich bags

1 oven bag (for roasting turkey or
chicken—large size) with tie

1 loaf pan

Heavy-duty aluminum foil

Wax paper

Kebab skewers (8)

Indelible marking pen

Freezer tape

Shopping List for Gluten-Free Two-Week Cycle by Categories

An asterisk (★) after an item in the shopping list indicates that the item will not be used until the day the entrée is served. When the item is fresh produce, such as a tomato, you may want to delay purchasing it until close to when you'll serve the dish. These items are all listed on the handy Menu Chart so you won't forget to purchase them before they're needed. Incorporate these into a weekly grocery shopping list so that you can continue to minimize trips to the store.

Produce

Carrots: 3 medium (1¼ cups chopped)

Celery: 1 stalk (⅓ cup chopped)

Cucumber: 1★

Garlic, cloves chopped: 1 jar (24 cloves needed)

Green bell pepper: 2 large

Lemons: 2 (1★)

Lettuce, romaine: 1 head★

Onions: 4 medium (3 chopped [5¾ cups], 1 cut in wedges)

Onions, red: 1 medium

Red potatoes, new: 8

Tomatoes: 1 large★

Dairy

Feta cheese, crumbled: 6 ounces

Parmesan cheese, gluten-free: ½ cup

Frozen

Artichokes, frozen: 1 8-ounce package (if not available, use canned)

Broccoli, frozen, chopped: 1 10-ounce package

Spinach, frozen, chopped: 1 10-ounce package

Meats, Poultry, Fish

Beef, ground lean: 3 pounds

Beef, London broil: 2 pounds

Chicken, boneless, skinless breast halves: 22

Chicken, whole roaster: 5 to 7 pounds

Ham shanks, smoked, or ham bone: 1½ to 2 pounds

Tuna steaks: 4 (6 ounces each)

Canned Goods

Beer, gluten-free: 1 12-ounce can★

Chicken broth, gluten-free: 1 14.5-ounce can

Chickpeas (garbanzos): 1 15-ounce can

Chili sauce: 1 12-ounce jar (1 cup needed)

Mandarin oranges: 1 11-ounce can

Mushrooms, pieces and stems: 2 8-ounce cans

Mushrooms, sliced: 1 7-ounce can

Olives, kalamata, pitted: 1 7-ounce jar

Olives, ripe, pitted and sliced: 1 2¼-ounce can

Pineapple, chunks: 1 20-ounce can

Pineapple juice, unsweetened:
2 6-fluid ounce cans (10-ounces
needed)

Tomatoes, diced: 2 14.5-ounce
cans

Tomatoes, diced, unsalted:
2 14.5-ounce cans

White beans (Great Northern
beans), unsalted: 1 14.5-ounce
can

Bakery

Kaiser rolls, gluten-free: 4

Pasta, Rice

Penne or mostaccioli, gluten-
free★: 1 pound package

Rice, brown: 1 32-ounce bag★:
(4½ cups needed)

Rice, white: 1 16-ounce bag
(½ cup needed)

Split peas: 1 16-ounce package

Seasonings

Bragg's Liquid Amino: 1 16-fluid
ounce bottle (1 cup needed)

Other

Cashews: ¾ cup needed

Peanuts, dry roasted: 1 cup needed

Sweet rice flour: 1 20-ounce box
(9 tablespoons needed)

Assembly Order for Gluten-Free Two-Week Cycle

Label freezer containers.

Processing

VEGETABLES

Celery: Chop 1 stalk (⅓ cup).

Carrots: Peel and chop 3 (1¼ cups).

Green bell pepper: Cut 1 in ¾-inch squares.

Lemon: Grate 1 tablespoon zest, squeeze 2 tablespoons juice.

Red onion: Slice ½ onion.

Onions: 4—Cut 1 into wedges for kebabs, chop 3 (5¾ cups).

Spinach: Thaw, drain, and squeeze dry 1 10-ounce box.

CHICKEN

With kitchen shears, cut 4 boneless, skinless chicken breast halves into ½-inch-wide strips.

With kitchen shears, cut 10 boneless, skinless chicken breast halves into 1½-inch cubes for Nanners Chicken Kebabs (2). Cashew Chicken (2), Slow Cooker Artichoke, Chicken, and Olives (2), and Honey Ginger Chicken Bites (4). Refrigerate these until needed, separated into bags.

BEEF

Prepare BBQ Roast and freeze.

Prepare Mediterranean Burgers and freeze.

Prepare Old-Fashioned Meat Loaf and freeze.

PORK

In a medium skillet sauté 2½ cups chopped onion and 3 chopped carrots in 2 tablespoons olive oil. When the onions are nearly transparent, remove a cup of the onion-carrot mixture for Vegan Creamy Tomato Soup. Add ⅓ cup sliced celery to the remaining onions and carrots in the skillet and continue sautéing until the onions are transparent.

Complete the Swedish Yellow Split Pea Soup and freeze.

SEAFOOD/MEATLESS

Put the reserved onions and carrots back in the skillet, add ½ teaspoon chopped garlic and sauté until the onion is transparent. Complete Vegan Creamy Tomato Soup and freeze.

Prepare Penne with Chickpeas and freeze.

Prepare Teriyaki Tuna Steaks and freeze.

You will be glad you did this. Your family will be, too.
One more group of recipes to go!

CHICKEN

Begin cooking chicken for Chicken à l'Orange.

Prepare Parsley, Sage, Rosemary, and Thyme Chicken and freeze.

Prepare Szechwan Chicken and Peanuts and freeze.

Prepare Cashew Chicken.

Prepare Slow Cooker Artichoke, Chicken, and Olives and freeze.

Prepare Honey-Ginger Chicken Bites and freeze.

Prepare Nanners Chicken Kebabs and freeze.

Complete Chicken à l'Orange and freeze.

Put your feet up and celebrate. You did it!

RECIPES FOR GLUTEN-FREE TWO-WEEK CYCLE

Consultant Lori Baird revised these recipes to fit the gluten-free lifestyle. Some are also dairy-free. Always carefully check each ingredient label when cooking gluten-free. If you are in doubt if a product is gluten-free, call or e-mail the company before buying it. Lori is dedicated to creating options for easy, healthy, delicious, allergy free meals. To learn and grow with Lori, visit her new Web site at www.eatingallergyfree.com. You will see a cooking demonstration of the Vegan Creamy Tomato Soup recipe she provided in this chapter on her Web site.

BBQ Roast

2 pounds London broil
1 cup (8 ounces) unsweetened
  pineapple juice
1½ teaspoons chopped garlic
2 tablespoons olive oil

1 teaspoon gluten-free Dijon
  mustard
⅓ cup red wine vinegar
2 tablespoons ketchup
1 tablespoon Bragg's Liquid Amino

Place the meat in a labeled 1-gallon freezer bag. Mix the remaining ingredients, pour over the meat, and freeze.

To serve, thaw the meat. Grill the meat to medium rare, or broil the meat at a high temperature, 3 inches from the heat source for 10 minutes per side.

Reduce the heat to 350°F (if broiling), and continue to cook for an additional 20 minutes. While cooking, baste with the leftover marinade, then discard the remainder (contains raw meat juices). Cut the meat in thin diagonal slices, against the grain.

SERVES 8

FREEZE IN: 1-gallon Ziploc freezer bag

Mediterranean Burgers

6 ounces crumbled feta cheese
1 teaspoon dried oregano
1 teaspoon dried rosemary
¾ teaspoon pepper, divided
1 lemon (1 tablespoon zest and 2
   tablespoons juice)
1½ pounds lean ground beef
½ cup pitted kalamata olives
1 tablespoon dried dill weed

1 tablespoon parsley flakes
¼ teaspoon sugar
3 tablespoons olive oil
4 Kaiser or other gluten-free
   sandwich rolls★
1 large sliced tomato★
¼ medium sliced cucumber★
½ medium sliced red onion★
8 romaine lettuce leaves★

In a bowl, combine the feta cheese, oregano, rosemary, ½ teaspoon pepper, and the lemon zest. Add the ground meat and mix gently. Form into four 1-inch-thick patties.

In a blender, whirl the olives, dill, parsley, lemon juice, sugar, and remaining ¼ teaspoon pepper. Add the olive oil, 1 tablespoon at a time, to make a smooth paste. Place the patties in a labeled 1-gallon freezer bag with wax paper between them. Put the olive sauce in a sandwich bag, slip it inside the bag with the patties, and freeze.

To serve, thaw the patties and sauce. Heat a gas grill to medium or charcoal grill to medium-hot coals. Grill the burgers, turning once, until browned on both sides and cooked through (cut to test); 10 to 12 minutes total. Split the rolls and toast, cut sides down, on the grill. Brush the toasted side with the olive mixture and garnish with tomato, cucumber, red onion, and lettuce leaves.

SUMMARY OF PROCESSES: Grate lemon for 1 tablespoon zest, squeeze 2 tablespoons juice.

SERVES 4

FREEZE IN: 1-gallon Ziploc freezer bag; 1 Ziploc sandwich bag; wax paper

Old-Fashioned Meat Loaf

1 teaspoon olive oil
1 cup chopped onion
2 teaspoons chopped garlic
1½ pounds lean ground beef
¾ cup old-fashioned oats, gluten-free
2 large egg whites

1 cup chili sauce, divided
½ teaspoon pepper
¼ teaspoon salt
1 tablespoon gluten-free Dijon
    mustard

Heat the oil in a large skillet over medium heat. Add the onion and sauté 5 minutes, stirring frequently. Add the garlic and cook 1 minute. Remove from heat and transfer to a large bowl. Let sit for 5 minutes. Add the beef, oats, egg whites, ½ cup chili sauce, pepper and salt, if desired. Mix well and pour into a 9×5-inch loaf pan treated with gluten-free cooking spray. Combine the remaining ½ cup chili sauce and mustard in small bowl; spoon evenly over top of meat loaf. Wrap in heavy-duty aluminum foil, label, and freeze.

To serve, thaw the meat loaf. Preheat the oven to 350°F. Bake the meat loaf 45 to 50 minutes. Let stand in the pan 5 minutes. Pour off any juices from pan. Cut into slices to serve.

SUMMARY OF PROCESSES: Chop 1 cup onion.

SERVES 6

FREEZE IN: Loaf pan; heavy-duty aluminum foil

Swedish Yellow Split Pea Soup

2 cups chopped onion
1 cup chopped carrots
⅓ cup chopped celery
1 tablespoon olive oil
1 pound yellow split peas
1½ to 2 pounds smoked ham
  shanks or ham bone

¾ teaspoon ground cardamom
¼ teaspoon marjoram
Dash cayenne pepper
1 can (12 ounces) gluten-free beer★
6 cups water★
1 tablespoon apple cider vinegar★
Salt to taste★

In a small skillet, sauté the onion, carrots, and celery in the olive oil, stirring occasionally, until the onion is soft but not browned. Meanwhile rinse and drain the split peas. Combine all ingredients through cayenne pepper in a labeled 1-gallon freezer bag and freeze. Store the marked can of beer in the refrigerator.

To serve, thaw the ingredients. Pour them into a large pot and add the beer and water. Bring to a boil, cover, reduce the heat, and simmer for 2½ to 3 hours, or until the ham and peas are tender.

Remove and discard the ham bones and rind. Return the meat to the soup in chunks. Stir in the vinegar. Salt to taste.

SUMMARY OF PROCESSES: Chop 2 cups onions; chop 1 cup carrots; chop ⅓ cup celery.

SERVES 6

FREEZE IN: 1-gallon Ziploc freezer bag

Penne with Chickpeas

1 10-ounce package frozen chopped
   spinach, thawed, drained, and
   squeezed dry
1/3 cup olive oil
3 teaspoons chopped garlic
1/4 teaspoon crushed red pepper flakes
1 14.5-ounce can diced tomatoes
1 15-ounce can chickpeas (or
   garbanzos), rinsed and drained

1/4 teaspoon salt
1/4 cup white wine
1/4 cup grated gluten-free Parmesan
   cheese*
1 pound gluten-free penne or
   mostaccioli (or other short,
   quill-shaped pasta)*

Place thawed, squeezed-dried spinach in a medium mixing bowl. Mix in the remaining ingredients through the wine, pour into a labeled 1-gallon freezer bag and freeze, attaching the sandwich bag with the Parmesan cheese. Store the marked pasta in the pantry.

To serve, place the thawed sauce in a large saucepan over medium heat until heated through. Cook the pasta according to package directions. Drain the pasta and stir into the sauce along with the Parmesan cheese.

SUMMARY OF PROCESSES: Thaw spinach and squeeze it dry.

SERVES 4

FREEZE IN: 1-gallon Ziploc freezer bag; 1 Ziploc sandwich bag

Vegan Creamy Tomato Soup*

¼ cup chopped carrot
¼ cup chopped onion
2 teaspoons chopped garlic
1 tablespoon extra virgin olive
  oil
2 14.5-ounce cans unsalted diced
  tomatoes

1 14.5-ounce can unsalted white
  beans (Great Northern beans),
  rinsed and drained
1 teaspoon dried tarragon, crushed
1 lemon (1 tablespoon lemon juice
  and 1 teaspoon lemon zest)*
Salt and pepper to taste*

In a skillet, sauté the carrot, onion, and garlic in the oil until translucent. Cool slightly and combine with the tomatoes, rinsed and drained beans, and tarragon in a labeled 1-gallon freezer bag. Freeze. Store lemon in a marked sandwich bag in the refrigerator.

To serve, thaw the soup. In a large pot, simmer over low heat for about ½ hour. Stir in the lemon juice, zest, and salt and pepper. Turn heat off and let the soup cool. Puree until smooth.

SUMMARY OF PROCESSES: Chop ¼ cup carrots and ¼ cup onion.

SERVES 4

FREEZE IN: 1-gallon Ziploc freezer bag, 1 Ziploc sandwich bag

*Free from: gluten wheat, casein, lactose dairy, soy, yeast, corn, egg, nuts, seafood shellfish, no added sugar, low in sodium.

Teriyaki Tuna Steaks

¼ cup Bragg's Liquid Amino sauce
3 tablespoons brown sugar
3 tablespoons olive oil
2 tablespoons distilled white vinegar
2 tablespoons dry sherry

2 tablespoons unsweetened pineapple
juice
1 teaspoon chopped garlic
1½ teaspoons ground ginger
4 tuna steaks (6 ounces each)

In a small bowl, combine all the ingredients except the tuna steaks. Pour the marinade into a labeled 1-quart freezer bag. Freeze the tuna steaks in a labeled 1-gallon freezer bag (if you bought the tuna steaks individually frozen, keep them in their packaging), and freeze with the smaller bag of marinade slipped inside the gallon bag.

To serve, thaw the ingredients. When the tuna steaks are beginning to thaw, cut off the packaging, and dry off the steaks with paper towels. Reserve about ⅓ of the marinade in a separate bowl in the refrigerator for basting later. Slip the tuna steaks into the remaining marinade. From this point be sure to thaw the fish in the refrigerator.

Coat the grill rack of a gas or charcoal grill with gluten-free cooking spray. Heat the gas grill to medium or or the charcoal grill to medium-hot coals. Grill the tuna, uncovered, over medium heat for 5 to 6 minutes on each side. Baste during cooking with the reserved marinade, then discard and used marinade (contains raw meat juices).

SERVES 4

FREEZE IN: 1-gallon Ziploc freezer bag; 1 quart Ziploc freezer bag

Chicken à l'Orange

8 boneless, skinless chicken breast
   halves
½ cup rice flour
2 teaspoons salt
1 teaspoon paprika

½ cup butter
2 cups orange juice
1 11-ounce can mandarin oranges,
   drained★
2 cups uncooked brown rice★

In a bag, dust the chicken lightly with the mixture of flour, salt, and paprika. In a skillet, sauté the chicken in the butter until golden brown on the outside and no longer pink in the center, turning once. You may have to do this in two batches; don't crowd the pan.

Cool chicken and place into a labeled 1-gallon freezer bag. Pour the orange juice into a 1-quart freezer bag. Tape the two bags together and freeze. Store the marked can of mandarin oranges and place in the pantry.

To serve, thaw the ingredients. Preheat the oven to 375°F. Cook the rice according to package instructions. Place the chicken breasts in a 13×9×2-inch baking dish treated with gluten-free cooking spray. Pour in the orange juice, cover, and bake 20 minutes. Uncover and continue cooking 10 minutes to reduce the liquid to a slightly thickened sauce. Add the oranges and heat 5 more minutes. Serve over cooked rice.

SERVES 8 to 12, depending on size of chicken breasts

FREEZE IN: 1-gallon Ziploc freezer bag; 1-quart Ziploc freezer bag

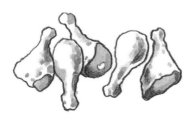

Parsley, Sage, Rosemary, and Thyme Chicken

1 5 to 7 pound whole roaster chicken
¼ cup olive oil
¼ cup gluten-free Parmesan cheese
1 tablespoon dried parsley
1 teaspoon ground sage
1 teaspoon dried thyme

1 teaspoon dried rosemary leaves
1 teaspoon chopped garlic
Salt and pepper to taste
¼ cup olive oil
1 teaspoon seasoned salt (optional)
1 tablespoon rice flour

Mix the first ¼ cup olive oil with the Parmesan cheese, parsley, sage, thyme, rosemary, and garlic. Rub the mixture on the chicken, getting it under the skin where possible. Then spread the second ¼ cup olive oil on the skin and sprinkle with the seasoned salt. Sprinkle the rice flour in the oven bag and shake to coat the bag. Slip the chicken into the labeled oven bag, close with the nylon tie (provided with the bag), and freeze.

To serve, thaw the chicken. Preheat the oven to 350°F. Place the bag with the chicken in a 13×9×2-inch baking dish. (The oven bag should not hang over the pan.) Cut six ½-inch slits in top. Place the pan in the oven, allowing room for the oven bag to expand during cooking without touching the oven walls or racks. Bake for 2 hours.

To serve, carefully cut open the top of the oven bag. Let chicken cool for 5 to 10 minutes before carving.

SERVES 6

FREEZE IN: 1 Oven bag (for roasting turkey or chicken)

Szechwan Chicken and Peanuts

4 boneless, skinless chicken breast
  halves
2 teaspoons cornstarch
¼ teaspoon ground ginger
2 tablespoons water
2 tablespoons dry sherry
¼ cup Bragg's Liquid Amino sauce
1 tablespoon sugar
1 tablespoon apple cider vinegar

1 teaspoon chopped garlic
½ to 1 teaspoon crushed red pepper
  flakes
1 green bell pepper, cut in ¾-inch
  squares
1 cup dry roast peanuts★
1 cup uncooked brown rice★
3 tablespoons vegetable oil★

Cut the chicken into ½-inch-wide strips and put in a labeled 1-gallon freezer bag. Mix the cornstarch, ginger, water, sherry, Bragg's Liquid Amino sauce, sugar, vinegar, and garlic until smooth and pour into a sandwich bag. Put the red pepper flakes into a second sandwich bag and the bell pepper squares into a third sandwich bag. Place the small bags into the 1-quart bag with the chicken and freeze. Store the marked container of dry roast peanuts in the pantry.

To serve, thaw the ingredients. Cook the rice according to package directions. Heat the oil in a large, heavy frying pan or wok placed over high heat. Add the crushed red pepper flakes and peanuts. Cook, stirring until the peanuts are browned. Drain the peanuts on paper towels.

Add the chicken strips to the pan and cook, stirring, until the chicken is white and opaque-looking throughout. Add the bell peppers and cook, stirring, about 2 minutes more. Stir in the Bragg's sauce mixture and add it to the chicken. Cook, stirring, until the sauce is thickened and clear. Return the peanuts to the pan and continue cooking until the bell peppers are tender-crisp. Served over the cooked rice.

SUMMARY OF PROCESSES: Cut 4 boneless, skinless chicken breast halves into ½-inch strips; cut 1 green bell pepper into ¾-inch squares.

SERVES 4

FREEZE IN: 1-gallon Ziploc freezer bag; 3 Ziploc sandwich bags

Cashew Chicken

2 boneless, skinless chicken breast
   halves, cubed
1 cup chopped onion
1 10-ounce package frozen, chopped
   broccoli
1 7-ounce can sliced mushrooms,
   drained

1 tablespoon chicken bouillon
½ to 1 teaspoon ground ginger
¾ cup cashews*
½ cup uncooked rice*

Combine the ingredients through the ginger in a bowl. Pour into a labeled 1-gallon freezer bag and freeze. Store the cashews in a labeled sandwich bag and attach to other bag.

To serve, thaw the ingredients. Transfer to a prepared, shallow 1½ quart baking dish that has been treated with gluten-free cooking spray. Stir in ½ cup cashews, and sprinkle the remaining ones on top. Cover and bake in a 375°F oven for 45 to 55 minutes. Meanwhile cook the rice according to package directions. Serve the cashew chicken over the rice.

SUMMARY OF PROCESSES: Cube 2 boneless, skinless chicken breasts; chop 1 cup onion.

SERVES 4

FREEZE IN: 1-gallon Ziploc freezer bag; 1 Ziploc sandwich bag

Slow Cooker Artichoke, Chicken, and Olives

2 cubed boneless, skinless chicken breast halves

2 8-ounce cans mushrooms pieces and stems, drained

1 14.5-ounce can diced tomatoes, undrained

1 8-ounce frozen (or canned) artichokes

1 14.5-ounce can gluten-free chicken broth

1 cup chopped onion

2 dashes gluten-free Tabasco sauce

1 2¼-ounce can sliced, pitted, ripe olives

¼ cup dry white wine

3 tablespoons quick-cooking tapioca

1 tablespoon curry powder

¾ teaspoon dried thyme, crushed

Salt and pepper to taste

1½ cups uncooked brown rice★

Combine all the ingredients, except the brown rice, in a large mixing bowl. Then pour them into a labeled 1-gallon freezer bag and freeze.

To serve, thaw the ingredients. Pour into a 3½-quart slow cooker. Cover and cook on low for 7 to 8 hours or on high for 3½ to 4 hours. Before serving, cook the rice according to package directions. Serve with cooked rice.

SUMMARY OF PROCESSES: Cube 2 boneless, skinless chicken breast halves; chop 1½ cups onion.

SERVES 6

FREEZE IN: 1-gallon Ziploc freezer bag

Honey-Ginger Chicken Bites

2⁄3 cup honey
2 teaspoons dried ginger
2 tablespoons lemon juice
2 tablespoons apple cider vinegar
2 tablespoons Bragg's Liquid Amino
   sauce
2 teaspoons dark sesame oil
1 teaspoon grated orange zest
   (optional and not on shopping list)

2 teaspoons chopped garlic
4 boneless, skinless chicken breast
   halves, cubed
2 teaspoons sesame seeds★
Gluten-free cooking spray★
1 teaspoon salt★
¼ teaspoon pepper★
2 teaspoons cornstarch★
2 teaspoons cold water★

Combine the first 8 ingredients in a labeled 1-gallon freezer bag; seal and shake well. Add the chicken, seal, and toss to coat. Pour the untoasted sesame seeds into a sandwich bag, attach to the larger bag and freeze.

To serve, thaw the ingredients. Preheat the oven to 425°F. Remove the chicken from the bag, reserving the marinade. Arrange the chicken in a single layer on the rack of a broiler pan coated with gluten-free cooking spray. Sprinkle the chicken with salt and pepper. Bake for 20 minutes, stirring once.

While the chicken is cooking, boil the marinade in a small saucepan for 3 minutes, stirring frequently. Combine the cornstarch and water in a small bowl and stir into the marinade. Cook 1 minute. Remove from the heat.

Remove the chicken from the oven and turn the oven control to broil. Spoon the glaze onto the chicken and toss well to coat. Place the chicken mixture back on the broiler rack; broil 5 minutes, or until browned, stirring twice. Meanwhile toast the sesame seeds in a small skillet on the stovetop over medium heat for approximately 5 minutes. Watch carefully as they will toast quickly. Sprinkle the chicken with the toasted sesame seeds.

SUMMARY OF PROCESSES: Cube 4 boneless, skinless chicken breast halves.

SERVES 6

FREEZE IN: 1-gallon Ziploc freezer bag; 1 Ziploc sandwich bag

Nanner's Chicken Kebabs

½ cup vegetable oil
¼ cup Bragg's Liquid Amino sauce
¼ cup gluten-free Dijon mustard
¼ cup lemon juice
1 teaspoon pepper
2 boneless, skinless chicken breast
  halves, cut into 1½-inch cubes

Kebabs:
8 new, red potatoes, parboiled before
  threading on kebabs★
1 20-ounce can pineapple chunks
1 onion, cut into wedges wide enough
  to pierce with a skewer★
1 green bell pepper, cut into wedges
  wide enough to pierce with
  a skewer★
8 kebab skewers★

Combine the marinade ingredients and chicken cubes in a labeled 1-gallon freezer bag, and freeze. Label and store the fresh ingredients for the kebabs in the refrigerator, or purchase closer to the day you'll serve the dish.

To serve, thaw the chicken cubes. Pour off and reserve the marinade. If desired, boil the potatoes, cut in half, for 10 minutes, or until just beginning to soften. Make kebabs with the halved new potatoes, pineapple chunks, onion wedges, bell pepper wedges, and chicken cubes, and grill on a gas grill at medium heat or a charcoal grill over medium-hot coals for approximately 12 minutes. Brush reserved marinade on the kebabs while you're cooking, then discard the remainder (contains raw meat juices).

SUMMARY OF PROCESSES: Cut 2 boneless, skinless chicken breast halves into 1½-inch cubes.

SERVES 4

FREEZE IN: 1-gallon Ziploc freezer bag

SUMMER TWO-WEEK CYCLE

Keep a lid on mealtime expenses, and enjoy a summer lifestyle long on grilling, picnics, and simpler meals.

Menu Chart for Summer Two-Week Cycle

RECIPE	SERVINGS	MEAT USED	METHOD	NEEDED TO SERVE	SERVE WITH
Barbie's Lettuce Wrap	4	Rotisserie chicken	Microwave	Cashews, bibb lettuce	
Chicken Enchiladas I	8	Rotisserie chicken	Slow cooker	Enchilada sauce, corn tortillas	
Barb's Wild Rice–Chicken Curry Salad	4	Rotisserie chicken		Mayonnaise, sliced almonds	
Hot Chicken and Green Chile Salad	6	Rotisserie chicken	Bake	Corn chips	
Orange Tarragon-Glazed Chicken	6	Boneless chicken breasts	Bake or grill		
Pesto Drumsticks	5	Chicken drumsticks	Grill or broil		
Freezer Coleslaw with Ham	6	Ham			
Red Rocks Ham Rolls	10	Ham	Bake		
Pork Barbecue	8	Pork Boston butt roast	Slow cooker	Sandwich buns	
Foil-Wrapped Fish Packets	4	Fish	Grill		
Grandma's Chili	6-8	Lean ground beef	Heat	Fritos, cheddar cheese	
Pepper Steak Stir-Fry	4	Beef flank steak	Stir-fry	Olive oil	
Steak Kebabs	8	Beef round steak	Broil or grill	Mushrooms	
Juicy Cookout Burgers	6	Lean ground beef	Grill	Lettuce, tomatoes	

PANTRY LIST FOR SUMMER TWO-WEEK CYCLE

Herbs and Spices

Cayenne pepper: 1 teaspoon

Celery seed: 1 teaspoon

Cumin, ground: ¼ teaspoon

Curry powder: 1½ teaspoons

Dry mustard: 3½ tablespoons

Garlic, chopped: 1 clove

Garlic powder: ¼ teaspoon

Garlic salt: ½ teaspoon

Ginger, ground: ¾ teaspoon

Mustard seed: 1 teaspoon

Onion powder: ½ teaspoon

Oregano: 1½ teaspoons

Pepper

Salt

Seasoned salt: 1 teaspoon

Tarragon, dried: 1 tablespoon

Other

Brown sugar: 9 tablespoons

Cooking spray

Dry sherry: 1 tablespoon

Honey: ⅓ cup

Ketchup: 1 cup

Lemon juice: 3 tablespoons

Mayonnaise: 1¼ cups

Mustard, prepared: ¼ cup

Olive oil: ⅔ cup

Soy sauce: 3 tablespoons

Sugar: 1 cup, 1 teaspoon

White vinegar: 2 cups

White wine vinegar: 1 teaspoon

Worcestershire sauce: ¾ cup

Freezing Supplies

12 1-gallon Ziploc freezer bags

2 1-quart Ziploc freezer bags

8 Ziploc sandwich bags

1 8-cup Ziploc freezer container

Heavy-duty aluminum foil

Wax paper

1 13×9×2-inch baking dish

Metal skewers

Indelible marking pen

Masking tape

SHOPPING LIST FOR SUMMER TWO-WEEK CYCLE BY CATEGORIES

An asterisk (★) after an item in the shopping list indicates that the item will not be used until the day the entrée is served. When the item is fresh produce, such as a tomato, you may want to delay purchasing it until close to when you'll served the dish. These items are all listed on the handy Menu Chart so you won't forget to purchase them before they're needed. Incorporate these into a weekly grocery shopping list so that you can continue to minimize trips to the store.

Produce

Cabbage: 1 medium head (about 2 pounds)

Carrots: 2 large (1 cup shredded)

Celery: 2 stalks (⅔ cup chopped)

Dried Cranberries: 1 6-ounce package (¼ cup needed)

Green bell peppers: 5

Green onions: 2 bunches (1¼ cups chopped)

Lettuce: 1 head Bibb★

Lettuce: 1 head iceberg★

Onions: 5 medium (9½ cups chopped)

Red bell pepper: 1

Tomatoes: 2 large★

Dairy

Cheddar cheese, mild, shredded:
1 24-ounce package (20 ounces needed)

Monterey Jack cheese, shredded:
1 16-ounce package (14 ounces needed)

Frozen

Orange juice concentrate:
1 12-ounce can

Vegetables, Garden Variety mixture such as cauliflower, carrots, and asparagus:
1 16-ounce bag

Meats, Poultry, Fish

Beef, flank steak: 1 pound

Beef, lean ground: 5 pounds

Beef, top round or boneless sirloin steak: 2 pounds

Chicken, boneless, skinless breast halves: 6

Chicken, drumsticks: 10

Chicken, roasted (rotisserie): 3 whole

Ham: 1⅓ pounds

Pork shoulder roast (Boston butt): 3 pounds

Orange roughy, individually frozen fillets: 4 (about 1 pound)

Canned Goods

Green chiles, diced: 3 4-ounce cans; 1 7-ounce can

Green chili sauce with pork (preferably Stokes): 1 15-ounce can

Green chili enchilada sauce: 1 28-ounce can

Kidney beans: 1 15-ounce can

Mushroom pieces and stems: 1 4-ounce can

Mushrooms, whole: 1 8-ounce can

Olives, large ripe, pitted, sliced: 2 6-ounce cans

Tomatoes, diced: 1 14.5-ounce can

Tomato sauce: 2 8-ounce cans

Tomato soup: 1 14.5-ounce can

Bakery

Hard rolls: 10

Sandwich buns: 14

Pasta, Rice

Uncle Ben's Long-Grain and Wild Rice: 1 6-ounce box

Seasonings

Teriyaki sauce: 1 10-ounce bottle (1 cup needed)

Other

Almonds, sliced: 1 2.5-ounce package (¼ cup needed)

Cashews: 1 15-ounce package★ (1 cup needed)

Chili seasoning (Williams, or your favorite brand): 2 1-ounce packages

Corn chips: 1 9.5-ounce bag (1 cup crushed needed)

Dry onion mushroom soup mix: 2-ounce box (1 envelope needed)

Fritos: 1 9.5-ounce bag

Italian salad dressing: ½ cup

Pesto with basil: 1 7-ounce carton

Tortillas, corn, soft: 12 count package★ (8 needed)

ASSEMBLY ORDER FOR SUMMER TWO-WEEK CYCLE

Label freezer containers.

Processing

VEGETABLES

Cabbage: Shred 1 medium head; combine cabbage and 1 teaspoon salt as directed for Freezer Coleslaw with Ham and set aside for 1 hour.

Carrots: Shred 2 (1 cup).

Celery: Chop 2 stalks (⅔ cups).

Green bell pepper: Chop 1½ (1¾ cup); cut 3 into 1-inch squares.

Green onions: Chop 12 onions (1¼ cups).

Onion: Chop 5 (9½ cups).

Red bell pepper: Cut 1 into 1-inch squares.

BREAD

Hard rolls: Slice tops off and scoop out insides (reserving for breadcrumbs, if desired).

CHICKEN

Roasted (rotisserie) chicken: Debone and shred 2 chickens (6 cups needed); debone and dice 1 chicken (3 cups).

PORK

Ham: Cube 4 cups.

BEEF

Flank steak: Cut into thin slices.

Top round steak/sirloin: Cut into 1-inch cubes.

Processing is the most time-consuming task. You've accomplished much!
Now start assembling entrées . . .

PORK

Complete Freezer Coleslaw with Ham and freeze.

Sauté 3½ cups chopped onions in 1 tablespoon olive oil. When transparent, put aside ⅓ cup for Orange Tarragon-Glazed Chicken. With the remainder, complete Red Rocks Ham Rolls and freeze.

Prepare Pork Barbecue and freeze.

CHICKEN

Cook long grain and wild rice according to package directions for Barb's Wild Rice Chicken Curry Salad.

While rice is cooking, prepare Barbie's Lettuce Wrap and freeze.

Set out container of orange juice concentrate to thaw slightly.

Prepare Chicken Enchiladas and freeze.

Prepare Hot Chicken and Green Chile Salad and freeze.

Prepare Orange Tarragon-Glazed Chicken and freeze.

Prepare Pesto Drumsticks and freeze.

Complete Barb's Wild Rice Chicken Curry Salad and freeze.

FISH/EGGS

Prepare Foil-Wrapped Fish Packets and freeze.

Be thinking: With whom could you share a meal this month?

BEEF

Prepare Grandma's Chili. While it simmers,

Prepare Pepper Steak Stir-Fry and freeze.

Prepare Steak Kebabs and freeze.

Prepare Juicy Cookout Burgers and freeze.

Complete Grandma's Chili and freeze.

Look at all those entrées in your freezer. Enjoy!

RECIPES FOR SUMMER TWO-WEEK CYCLE

Freezer Coleslaw with Ham

1 medium head shredded cabbage
  (about 2 pounds)
1 teaspoon salt
1 cup sugar
1 cup white vinegar
¼ cup water

1 teaspoon celery seed
1 teaspoon mustard seed
1 cup shredded carrots
½ cup chopped green bell pepper
2 cups cubed ham

In a large bowl, combine the cabbage and salt and let stand for 1 hour. In a saucepan, combine the sugar, vinegar, water, celery seed, and mustard seed. Bring to a boil; boil 1 minute. Remove from the heat and cool.

Drain the cabbage if necessary. Add the carrot, bell pepper, and vinegar mixture. Transfer to a labeled 1-gallon freezer bag. Package the ham in a 1-quart freezer bag and tape to the cabbage bag.

Remove the coleslaw from the freezer 2 hours before serving. Serve with a slotted spoon.

SUMMARY OF PROCESSES: Cube 2 cups ham; shred 1 medium head cabbage and 2 large carrots; chop ½ cup bell pepper.

SERVES 6

FREEZE IN: 1-gallon Ziploc freezer bag; 1 quart Ziploc freezer bag

Red Rocks Ham Rolls

3 cups chopped onion
1 tablespoons olive oil
2 cups cubed ham
3 cups (12 ounces) shredded cheddar
cheese
1 6-ounce can pitted, sliced, ripe
olives

1 4-ounce can chopped green
chiles
½ cup ketchup
2 tablespoons lemon juice
10 hard rolls (about 4 inches
long)

In a skillet, sauté the chopped onion in the olive oil until transparent. Mix all the ingredients except the rolls and set aside. Slice the tops off the hard rolls and scoop out insides (save for breadcrumbs, if desired). Fill the hollowed rolls with the ham–cheese mixture. Replace the tops on the rolls and wrap individually in foil. Package in a labeled 1-gallon freezer bag and freeze.

To serve, thaw the bag of rolls. Place the foil-wrapped sandwiches on a baking sheet and bake in a very slow oven (275°F) for 1 hour. Wrap the foil-wrapped sandwiches in newspaper or a heavy towel to keep them warm as you take them to your picnic site.

SUMMARY OF PROCESSES: Cube 2 cups ham; chop 3 cups onion; slice tops off rolls and scoop out insides.

SERVES 10 sandwiches

FREEZE IN: Heavy-duty aluminum foil; 1-gallon Ziploc freezer bag

Pork Barbecue

3 pound Boston butt roast (pork
   shoulder)
2 cups chopped onion
3 tablespoons dry mustard
3 tablespoons brown sugar
¼ teaspoon pepper

1 teaspoon cayenne pepper
1 cup white vinegar
1½ cup water
½ cup ketchup
½ cup Worcestershire sauce
8 sandwich buns★

Pour all the ingredients except for the sandwich buns into a labeled 1-gallon freezer bag and freeze. Freeze the buns attached.

To serve, pour the contents of the bag into a slow cooker and simmer 5 to 6 hours or until thoroughly cooked. Shred the pork and remove the bone. Serve over warmed buns.

SUMMARY OF PROCESSES: Chop 2 cups onion.

SERVES 8

FREEZE IN: 1-gallon Ziploc freezer bag

Barb's Wild Rice–Chicken Curry Salad

1 6-ounce package Uncle Ben's
    Long-Grain and Wild Rice
2 cups deboned and shredded
    rotisserie chicken
¼ cup chopped celery
¼ cup chopped green onion

¼ cup dried cranberries
1½ teaspoons curry powder
1 teaspoon lemon juice
⅔ cups mayonnaise*
¼ cup toasted sliced almonds*

Cook the wild rice according to package directions. Meanwhile combine remaining ingredients, except mayonnaise and almonds, in a small mixing bowl. Add the wild rice, package in a labeled gallon bag, and freeze, with almonds in a sandwich bag attached. Store mayonnaise in refrigerator.

To serve, thaw mixture. Toast almonds spread in a pie tin in preheated 350°F oven for 5 to 8 minutes. Stir mayonnaise into curry-chicken mixture. Sprinkle with toasted almonds.

SUMMARY OF PROCESSES: Debone and shred 2 cups rotisserie chicken; chop ¼ cup celery; chop ¼ cup green onion.

SERVES 4

FREEZE IN: 1 gallon Ziploc freezer bag; 1 Ziploc sandwich bag

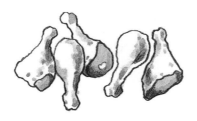

Barbie's Lettuce Wrap

1 cup teriyaki sauce
⅓ cup honey
½ cup chopped green onions
2 cups deboned and shredded
   rotisserie chicken

1 cup cashews★
1 head Bibb lettuce★

Put the teriyaki sauce, honey, and chopped green onions in a sandwich bag. Place the shredded chicken in a labeled 1-gallon freezer bag. Pour the cashews into another sandwich bag. Slip the sandwich bags into the gallon bag with the chicken, and freeze.

To serve, thaw the ingredients. Heat sauce for 20 seconds in a microwave-safe bowl, then pour over the chicken. Sprinkle with cashews. Fill individual lettuce leaves with the mixture, wrap, and serve immediately.

SUMMARY OF PROCESSES: Debone and shred 2 cups rotisserie chicken; chop ½ cup green onions.

SERVES 4

FREEZE IN: 1-gallon Ziploc freezer bag; 2 Ziploc sandwich bags

Chicken Enchiladas

2 cups chopped onion
1 4-ounce can mushrooms pieces and
  stems, drained
2 4-ounce cans chopped mild green
  chiles
1 6-ounce can pitted, sliced ripe olives
2 cups deboned and shredded
  rotisserie chicken

1 15-ounce can green chile sauce
  with pork (preferably Stokes)
2½ cups (10 ounces) shredded
  Monterey Jack cheese
1 28-ounce jar green chili enchilada
  sauce★
8 soft corn tortillas★

To a medium mixing bowl, add the onions, mushrooms, green chiles, olives, chicken, green chile sauce with pork, and stir to combine. Pour this mixture into a labeled 1-gallon freezer bag. Place the shredded Monterey Jack cheese in a sandwich bag, attach to the larger bag, and freeze. Store the marked package of tortillas in the refrigerator, and the marked jar of green chile en-chilada sauce in the pantry.

To serve, thaw the chicken mixture and the cheese. Pour half of the green chile enchilada sauce into a slow cooker. Spoon a line of the chicken mixture along the side of each tortilla. Roll the tortillas and place them in the slow cooker, stacking them at different angles. Cover with the remaining green chile sauce. Top with the cheese. Cook on low 6 to 8 hours.

SUMMARY OF PROCESSES: Debone and shred 2 cups rotisserie chicken; chop 2 cups onions.

SERVES 8

FREEZE IN: 1-gallon Ziploc freezer bag; 1 Ziploc sandwich bag

Hot Chicken and Green Chile Salad

½ cup mayonnaise
2 teaspoons lemon juice
1 teaspoon white wine vinegar
½ teaspoon dry mustard
½ teaspoon garlic salt
¼ teaspoon ground cumin
3 cups deboned and diced rotisserie chicken

⅓ cup chopped celery
½ cup chopped green onions
1 7-ounce can chopped green chiles
1 cup (4 ounces) shredded Monterey Jack
1 cup (4 ounces) shredded cheddar cheese
1 cup crushed corn chips★

For dressing, mix the mayonnaise, lemon juice, vinegar, mustard, garlic salt, and cumin until smooth. Lightly combine the dressing, chicken, celery, green onions, green chiles, and cheese. Pour into a labeled 1-gallon freezer bag and freeze. Store the marked bag of corn chips in the pantry.

To serve, thaw the chicken mixture. Divide the chicken mixture into 4 to 6 buttered, shallow, individual baking dishes. Top with the crushed corn chips. Bake, uncovered, in a preheated 400°F oven for 15 to 25 minutes, or until they are bubbly and heated through.

SUMMARY OF PROCESSES: Debone and dice 3 cups rotisserie chicken; chop ⅓ cup celery; chop ½ cup green onions.

SERVES 6

FREEZE IN: 1-gallon Ziploc freezer bag

Orange Tarragon-Glazed Chicken

½ cup chopped onion

2 teaspoons olive oil (optional, see directions)

6 medium boneless, skinless chicken breast halves

1 12-ounce container frozen orange juice concentrate, thawed slightly

1 tablespoon dried tarragon

1 teaspoon salt

In a skillet, sauté the onion in 2 teaspoons olive oil (or with onions for Red Rocks Ham Rolls). Pour all the ingredients, including the chicken, in a labeled 1-gallon freezer bag and freeze.

To serve, thaw the ingredients and pour into a 13×9×2-inch baking dish. Bake at 375°F for 50 minutes. Or grill the chicken on a gas grilled heated to medium heat for 20 minutes, or a charcoal grill over medium-hot coals, turning once.

SUMMARY OF PROCESSES: Chop ½ cup onions.

SERVES: 6

FREEZE IN: 1-gallon Ziploc freezer bag

Pesto Drumsticks

10 chicken drumsticks   *1 7-ounce carton pesto sauce with basil*

Lay out the chicken on a clean surface, pull the skin back from the top of the drumstick towards the end bone. Slather the meat with the pesto, and gently pull the skin back up over the pesto. Place chicken in a prepared 13×9×2-inch baking dish, cover with heavy-duty aluminum foil, label, and freeze.

To serve, thaw the drumsticks and grill over medium-hot coals, a gas grill heated to medium, or broil for approximately 20 minutes, turning once.

SERVES 5

FREEZE IN: 1 13×9×2-inch baking dish; heavy-duty aluminum foil

Foil-Wrapped Fish Packets

4 individually frozen orange roughy
    fillets (about 1 pound)
2 cups Garden Variety vegetable
    mixture with cauliflower, carrots,
    and asparagus (or similar
    vegetable mixture)

½ cup Italian salad
    dressing

Place each fish fillet on a large square of double-thickness, heavy-duty aluminum foil. Top each fillet with ½ cup of the vegetable mixture. Drizzle 2 tablespoons of Italian salad dressing over each. Wrap each packet securely with double-fold seal. Put the packets in a labeled 1-gallon freezer bag, and freeze.

To serve, keep the fillets frozen. A half hour before grilling them set them out to thaw slightly. Place the packets on gas grill over medium heat or on charcoal grill 4 to 6 inches from medium-hot coals. Cook, covered, 15 to 25 minutes, or until fish flakes easily with a fork and vegetables are hot. Rearrange the packets once halfway through the cooking. These packets may also be cooked on a campfire.

SERVES 4

FREEZE IN: heavy-duty aluminum foil; 1 gallon Ziploc freezer bag

Grandma's Chili

3 pounds lean ground beef
2 cups chopped onion
1⅓ cups chopped green bell pepper
1 teaspoon salt
¼ teaspoon pepper
½ teaspoon onion powder
¼ teaspoon garlic powder
1 15-ounce can kidney beans,
    undrained

1 14.5-ounce can diced tomatoes
1 8-ounce can tomato sauce
1 14.5-ounce can tomato soup
2 packages Williams (or your
    favorite) chili seasoning
⅓ cup packed brown sugar
1 small bag Fritos (optional)★
1 cup (4 ounces) shredded cheddar
    cheese (optional)★

Brown ground beef in a skillet and drain excess fat. Puree the onion and bell pepper in a blender with a little water. Add to the meat along with the remaining ingredients except Fritos and cheese. Simmer for 15 minutes. Cool and freeze in a labeled 8-cup freezer container. Freeze cheese in a sandwich bag attached to this container. Store the marked bag of Fritos in the pantry.

To serve, thaw the chili. In a saucepan bring the chili to a boil. Reduce heat and simmer at least 30 minutes. Pass Fritos and cheddar cheese.

SUMMARY OF PROCESSES: Chop 2 cups onion; chop 1⅓ cups green bell pepper.

SERVES 6 to 8

FREEZE IN: 8-cup Ziploc freezer container, 1 Ziploc sandwich bag

Pepper Steak Stir-Fry

1 pound flank steak, cut into thin
   strips
1 tablespoon dry sherry
3 tablespoons soy sauce
1 teaspoon sugar
1 medium green bell pepper, cut into
   1-inch squares

1 medium red bell pepper, cut into
   1-inch squares
1 clove chopped garlic
¾ teaspoon ground ginger
4 tablespoons olive oil, divided★

Cut the flank steak across the grain into thin slices. In a medium bowl, mix the wine, soy sauce, and sugar. Add the steak slices and mix to coat them thoroughly. Pour the steak mixture into a labeled 1-quart freezer bag.

Package the green and red bell peppers in a sandwich bag, and the garlic and ginger in another sandwich bag. Attach all 3 bags together, and freeze.

To serve, thaw the three packages. Heat a wok over high heat. Add 1 tablespoon olive oil and heat 30 seconds. Add the bell peppers to the hot oil and stir-fry about 3 minutes. Remove with slotted spoon and set aside.

Add the remaining 3 tablespoons olive oil to the wok and heat. Add the ginger and garlic, and a few seconds later, add the steak. Stir-fry over high heat for 2 minutes, or until there is no red showing. Return the bell peppers to the wok, and cook 1 minute more.

SUMMARY OF PROCESSES: Cut steak into thin strips; cut 1 green and 1 red bell pepper into 1-inch squares.

SERVES 4

FREEZE IN: 1-quart Ziploc freezer bag; 2 Ziploc sandwich bags

Steak Kebabs

2 pounds top round steak or boneless sirloin, cut into 1-inch cubes

Marinade:
¼ cup olive oil
¼ cup prepared yellow mustard
¼ cup Worcestershire sauce
1 teaspoon seasoned salt
1½ teaspoons dried oregano

2 green bell peppers, cut into 1-inch squares
1 8-ounce can whole mushrooms*

Pour the steak cubes into labeled 1-gallon freezer bag. Stir together the marinade ingredients and pour around the steak. Seal the green bell peppers in a sandwich bag and attach it to the bag with the steak and marinade. Store the marked can of mushrooms in the pantry.

To serve, thaw the ingredients. On metal skewers, alternate the meat, bell peppers, and mushrooms. Broil or grill 10 minutes over coals heated to medium heat or until meat is cooked, basting frequently with the marinade. Discard any remaining marinade.

SUMMARY OF PROCESSES: Cut 2 pounds round steak into 1-inch cubes; cut 2 green bell peppers into 1-inch squares.

SERVES 8

FREEZE IN: 1-gallon Ziploc freezer bag; 1 Ziploc sandwich bag

Juicy Cookout Burgers

2 pounds lean ground beef
1-ounce envelope dry onion
   mushroom soup mix
1 8-ounce can tomato sauce

6 sandwich buns
Lettuce leaves★
2 large sliced tomatoes★

In large bowl, combine the ground beef, soup mix, and tomato sauce and mix gently. Shape the mixture into 6 patties. Wrap each pattie in wax paper. Place the patties in a labeled 1-gallon freezer bag, and freeze. Freeze the buns in another 1-gallon freezer bag, and tape to the bag of patties.

To serve, preheat a grill. Place the patties on gas grill over medium heat or on charcoal grill 4 to 6 inches from medium-hot coals. Cook 14 to 19 minutes until no longer pink, turning once.

Toast the sandwich buns, cut side down, while the patties cook. Place a lettuce leaf on each bun; top with a tomato slice and a burger.

SERVES 6

FREEZE IN: Waxed paper; 2 1-gallon Ziploc freezer bags

GOURMET TWO-WEEK CYCLE

*D*elicious and elegant, these entrées will surprise even you to have come from your freezer.

Menu Chart for Gourmet Two-Week Cycle

RECIPE	SERVINGS	MEAT USED	METHOD	NEEDED TO SERVE	SERVE WITH
Green Chicken with Lemon-Pistachio Rice	4	Boneless chicken breasts	Bake	Rice, yogurt, lemon juice, pistachios,	
Southwest Chicken Pie	6	Boneless chicken breasts	Heat	Monterey Jack cheese	
Chicken to Go	4	Boneless chicken breasts	Bake		
Grilled Southwest Chicken with Cilantro Sauce	4	Boneless chicken breasts	Grill or bake	Monterey Pepper-Jack cheese, black beans, salsa	
Ham and Winter Vegetable Potpie	4–5	Ham steak	Bake	Pie crust, butter, flour	
Spicy Korean Pork Barbecue	4	Pork tenderloin	Grill		
Pork Roast with Apples and Mushrooms	12–14	Pork loin roast	Bake	Whipping cream, butter, apples, mushrooms	
Penne in Cream Sauce with Sausage	6	Italian sausage	Heat	Penne pasta, Parmesan cheese	
Corn Soup with Basil, Avocado, and Crab	4	Crabmeat		Milk, half-and-half, crabmeat, avocado, basil	
Five-Cheese Spinach Quiche	6	Meatless	Bake		
Red Mesa Tacos	9	Lean ground beef	Heat	Taco shells, lettuce, cheese, tomato, sour cream	
Uptown Joes	6–8	Lean ground round	Heat	Hamburger buns	
Peperoncini Pepper Roast	8	Beef roast	Slow cooker	Peperoncini peppers	
Orange Beef and Broccoli Stir-Fry	6	Flank steak	Stir fry	Broccoli, rice	

Pantry List for Gourmet Two-Week Cycle

Herbs and Spices

Basil leaves: 1 tablespoon crushed (3 tablespoons fresh)

Cayenne pepper: ¼ teaspoon

Cinnamon, ground: ½ teaspoon

Crushed red pepper: ½ teaspoon

Cumin, ground: 1 teaspoon

Dill weed: 1 teaspoon (1 tablespoon fresh)

Garlic powder: 1 teaspoon

Ginger, ground: ½ teaspoon (1 teaspoon fresh)

Oregano: 1 teaspoon (1 tablespoon fresh)

Pepper

Poppy seeds: 2½ teaspoons

Salt

Sesame seeds: 2½ tablespoons

Tarragon, dried: 1½ teaspoons (¼ cup fresh)

Thyme, ground: 2 tablespoons plus 1 teaspoon

Other

Brown sugar (light): ⅔ cup

Butter: 12 tablespoons (1½ sticks)

Cooking spray

Cornstarch: 3 tablespoons

Eggs: 6

Flour: 1¼ cups

Ketchup: 2 cups

Mustard, Dijon: ½ cup

Lemon juice: 2 teaspoons

Olive oil: ½ cup

Sesame oil, dark: 1 teaspoon

Sherry: ¼ cup

Soy sauce: ⅓ cup

Sugar: ⅔ cup

Tabasco sauce: 5 dashes

Vegetable oil: ¼ cup

Worcestershire sauce: ½ cup

Freezing Supplies

11 1-gallon Ziploc freezer bags

4 1-quart Ziploc freezer bags

7 Ziploc sandwich bags

2 8-cup Ziploc freezer containers

1 quiche pan

Heavy-duty aluminum foil

Freezer tape

Indelible marking pen

SHOPPING LIST FOR TWO-WEEK GOURMET BY CATEGORIES

An asterisk (★) after an item in the shopping list indicates that the item will not be used until the day the entrée is served. When the item is fresh produce, such as a tomato, you may want to delay purchasing it until close to when you'll served the dish. These items are all listed on the handy Menu Chart so you won't forget to purchase them before they're needed. Incorporate these into a weekly grocery shopping list so that you can continue to minimize trips to the store.

Produce

Apples★: 4 small cooking (2 cups wedges)

Avocado★: 1

Broccoli, fresh★: 12-ounces

Carrots: 4 medium (2 cups chopped)

Celery: 3 stalks (1 cup chopped)

Cilantro, fresh: 1 bunch (¼ cup chopped)

Garlic, chopped: 1 jar (17 cloves needed)

Green onions: 1 bunch (1 cup chopped)

Lemon: 1

Lettuce★: ½ head

Limes: 2

Mushrooms★: 2 cups sliced

Onions: 4 medium (1-2 cups sliced, 3-5 cups chopped)

Parsley: 1 bunch (½ cup chopped)

Parsnips: 3 (2 cups chopped)

Pistachio nuts: ¼ cup chopped

Potatoes: 3

Red bell pepper: 1 (½ cup chopped)

Tomato★: 1

Dairy

Cheddar cheese, mild, shredded:
1-12-ounce package (10 ounces
needed)

Cottage cheese: 1 8-ounce package
(1 cup needed)

Feta cheese, crumbled: 6 ounces

Gorgonzola cheese, crumbled:
5 ounces

Half-and-half: ½ pint (½ cup
needed)

Milk, 2 percent: ½ pint (½ cup
needed)

**Monterey Pepper-Jack cheese,
shredded:** 1 12-ounce package

Parmesan cheese, grated: 1½ cups

Sour cream: 1 24-ounce carton

Whipping cream: 1 pint (1 cup
needed)

Yogurt, plain: 2 6-ounce containers

Frozen

Corn, whole kernel, frozen:
32-ounce package (4 cups needed)

Peas, frozen: 8 ounce package
(1 cup needed)

Spinach, chopped: 1 10-ounce box,
1 16-ounce bag

Meats, Poultry, Fish

Beef, chuck roast: 2½ pounds

**Beef, lean ground (80 percent
lean):** 2 pounds

**Beef, ground round (90 percent
lean):** 2 pounds

**Chicken, boneless, skinless breast
halves:** 16

Flank steak: 1½ pounds

Ham steak: 1½ pounds

Italian sausage, hot: ½ pound

Italian sausage, mild: 1 pound

Pork loin roast: 3 to 4 pounds

Pork tenderloin: 1 pound

Canned Goods

Apple juice: ½ cup

Black beans: 2 15-ounce cans

Chicken broth: 2 32-ounce cartons,
 1 14.5-ounce can

Crabmeat, lump: 1 6-ounce can

Kidney beans: 2 15-ounce cans

Marmalade, orange: 8 ounces

Mexicorn: 1 11-ounce can (whole
 kernel corn with red and green
 pepper)

Olives, ripe, pitted and sliced:
 1 2¼-ounce can

Peperoncini peppers: 1 16-ounce
 jar★

Salsa: 16-ounce jar (2 cups needed)

Tomato sauce: 1 15-ounce can

Tomatoes, diced: 3 14.5-ounce
 cans

Bakery

Round crusty peasant loaf: 1★

Hamburger buns: 6 to 8

Hard rolls: 8★

Pasta, Rice

Mini penne pasta: 1 pound

Rice: 2½ cups, uncooked

Seasonings

Hoisin sauce: ¼ cup (Asian section)

McCormick's Chili Seasoning Mix: 2 packages

Thai chile paste: 1½ tablespoons (Asian section)

Other

Dry white wine: ⅔ cup

Piecrust: 1 9-inch Pillsbury

Corn taco shell: 1 package

Dry sherry: ¼ cup

ASSEMBLY ORDER FOR GOURMET TWO-WEEK CYCLE

Label freezer containers.

Processing

HERBS

Fresh cilantro: Chop ¼ cup.

Fresh parsley: Chop ½ cup.

FRUITS AND VEGETABLES

Carrots: Peel and chop 4 medium (2 cups).

Celery: Chop 3 stalks (1 cup chopped).

Green onions: Chop 1 cup.

Lemon: 1 Grate 2 teaspoons zest, squeeze 3 tablespoons juice.

Limes: 2 Squeeze juice

Onion, medium: Slice 1 (2 cups); chop 3 (5 cups)

Parsnips: Peel and chop 3 (2 cups).

Potatoes: Peel and chop 3.

Red bell pepper: Chop ½ cup.

Spinach: 1 10-ounce package and 1 16-ounce package—Thaw, drain, and squeeze dry.

NUTS

Shell and chop ¼ cup pistachios.

CHICKEN

Boneless, skinless breast halves: Cut 8 breast halves into ½-inch strips for Adobe Chicken and Chicken to Go.

PORK

Ham steak: Debone and trim fat; cut meat into cubes.

Tenderloin: Cut 1 pound into ¼-inch slices, diagonally, against the grain.

BEEF

Slice flank steak into ½-inch strips.

Processing is the most time-consuming task. You've accomplished much!
Now start assembling dishes . . .

CHICKEN

Prepare and freeze Green Chicken with Lemon-Pistachio Rice.

Prepare and freeze Adobe Chicken.

In a large skillet, cook chicken for Chicken to Go, meanwhile

Prepare Grilled Southwest Chicken with Cilantro Sauce and freeze.

Complete Chicken to Go and freeze.

PORK

Prepare Ham and Winter Vegetable Potpie and freeze.

Prepare Spicy Korean Pork Barbecue and freeze.

Prepare Pork Roast with Apples and Mushrooms and freeze.

Prepare Penne in Cream Sauce with Sausage and freeze.

EGGS/SEAFOOD

Prepare Corn Soup with Basil, Avocado, and Crab and freeze.

Prepare Five Cheese–Spinach Quiche and freeze.

BEEF

Prepare and simmer Red Mesa Tacos, meanwhile

Prepare and freeze Uptown Joes.

Prepare Peperoncini Pepper Roast and freeze.

Prepare and freeze Orange Beef and Broccoli Stir-Fry.

Complete and freeze Red Mesa Tacos.

Celebrate—you did it!

RECIPES FOR GOURMET TWO-WEEK CYCLE

Green Chicken with Lemon-Pistachio Rice

1 cup chicken broth
1 10-ounce package frozen chopped
    spinach, thawed, drained, and
    squeezed dry
1 14.5-ounce can diced tomatoes
1 lemon (2 teaspoons zest, 2
    tablespoons juice)
1 teaspoon dried oregano
    (1 tablespoon chopped fresh)

1 teaspoon dried dill weed
    (1 tablespoon snipped fresh)
½ teaspoon ground cinnamon
¼ teaspoon pepper
4 boneless, skinless chicken breast halves
1 cup uncooked rice★
¼ cup chopped pistachios★
1 6-ounce carton plain yogurt★
2 teaspoons lemon juice★

FRESH OREGANO AND dill weed may also be used as an optional garnish—they are not on the shopping list.

In a medium bowl, stir together the broth, spinach, tomatoes, lemon zest, 2 tablespoons lemon juice, and spices. Place the chicken breast halves in a labeled 1-gallon freezer bag and pour the sauce over them. Attach a sandwich bag with ¼ cup chopped pistachios, and freeze. Mark the yogurt container and store in the refrigerator.

To serve, thaw the green chicken mixture. Pour into a 13×11×2-inch baking dish, cover with foil, and bake in a preheated 375°F oven for 50 to 60 minutes.

Stir together the yogurt and 2 teaspoons lemon juice and spoon over the chicken. Sprinkle with ¼ cup chopped pistachios and serve.

SUMMARY OF PROCESSES: Thaw, drain, and squeeze dry package of frozen spinach; grate 2 teaspoons lemon zest and squeeze 2 tablespoons lemon juice.

SERVES 4

FREEZE IN: 1-gallon Ziploc freezer bag; 1 Ziploc sandwich bag

Adobe Chicken

4 boneless, skinless chicken breast
  halves, cut into ½-inch strips
2 tablespoons olive oil
½ teaspoon salt
½ teaspoon pepper
1 15-ounce can black beans, drained,
  rinsed
1 11-ounce Mexicorn (whole kernel
  corn with red and green peppers),
  drained

1 2¼-ounce can pitted, sliced ripe
  olives, drained
1 teaspoon garlic powder
1 teaspoon ground cumin
1 cup (8 ounces) sour cream
1 cup salsa
2 cups (8 ounces) shredded Monterey
  Pepper-Jack Cheese*

With kitchen shears, cut 4 chicken breast halves into strips. Cook the strips in a skillet in the olive oil, turning frequently. Season the chicken strips with salt and pepper as they cook.

Meanwhile, in a large bowl, mix all the remaining ingredients except the cheese. Pour the chicken strips and mixture into a labeled 1-gallon freezer bag and tape to it a sandwich bag filled with the grated cheese.

To serve, thaw the chicken mixture and cheese. Place the chicken in a deep skillet. Bring to a boil, reduce heat, and simmer 10 minutes. Sprinkle the cheese over chicken to serve.

SUMMARY OF PROCESSES: Cut 4 chicken breast halves in strips.

SERVES 6

FREEZE IN: 1-gallon Ziploc freezer bag; 1 Ziploc sandwich bag

Chicken to Go

1 cup all-purpose flour
1½ tablespoons sesame
   seeds
1½ teaspoons dried thyme
2 teaspoons dried tarragon
1½ teaspoons poppy seeds
1 teaspoon salt
4 boneless, skinless chicken
   breast halves, cut into ½-inch
   strips
2 lightly beaten eggs
¼ cup olive oil

Herb Butter:
6 tablespoons butter
1 tablespoon sesame seeds
½ teaspoon dried tarragon
1 teaspoon dried thyme
1 teaspoon poppy seeds

1 round crusty peasant loaf

In a small mixing bowl, combine the flour, sesame seeds, thyme, tarragon, poppy seeds, and salt. Dip the chicken breast strips in the beaten eggs, and then coat each piece in the flour mixture. In a large skillet, heat the olive oil. Brown chicken thoroughly in the oil over medium heat. Cool the chicken and package in a labeled 1-gallon bag. Meanwhile, mix together the Herb Butter ingredients, and put into a sandwich bag. Put the sandwich bag into another freezer bag with the loaf of peasant bread. Tape the two bags together, and freeze.

To serve, thaw the chicken. In small saucepan, heat the herb butter ingredients until the butter is melted. Keep warm.

Cut the top off the peasant loaf. Scrape out the inside of loaf, leaving about a ¾-inch shell all the way around the inside. Using a pastry brush, spread the Herb Butter inside the loaf and on the inside of the top. Place the loaf and top on a cookie sheet. Arrange the chicken in the loaf. Put in the oven and bake, uncovered, at 350°F for 30 minutes or until heated through. Remove the loaf from the oven. Serve the chicken, or replace the top and wrap in several layers of foil, surrounded by several layers of newspaper, to transport to a picnic or a friend.

SUMMARY OF PROCESSES: Cut 4 chicken breast halves into ½-inch strips.

SERVES 4

FREEZE IN: 2 1-gallon Ziploc freezer bags (one for bread loaf); 1 Ziploc sandwich bag

Grilled Southwest Chicken
with Cilantro Sauce

4 boneless, skinless chicken breast
   halves
1 lime
1 teaspoon chopped garlic

Cilantro Sauce:
1 6-ounce container plain yogurt
1 cup (8 ounces) sour cream
¼ cup chopped fresh cilantro
1 lime
½ teaspoon salt
½ teaspoon pepper
1 cup (4 ounces) shredded Monterey
   Pepper-Jack Cheese★
1 15-ounce can black beans★
1 cup salsa★

Place the chicken breasts on a cutting board. Coat both sides of the chicken breasts with the juice of 1 lime. Take the garlic and rub into both sides of the chicken breasts evenly. Let the chicken stand for approximately 5 minutes while you prepare the Cilantro Sauce.

Mix together the yogurt, sour cream, and fresh cilantro. Add the juice of the second lime. Add the salt and pepper and mix well. Place the chicken in a labeled 1-gallon freezer bag. Put the cilantro sauce in a 1-quart freezer bag, and the shredded cheese in a sandwich bag. Tape or clip the three bags together, label, and freeze.

To serve, thaw the contents of all bags. Heat a grill (or oven to 375°F). Place the chicken on the grill (or in the oven), and let cook for 5 to 6 minutes on the grill (50 minutes in the oven). The internal temperature when measured with a thermometer should register 162°F or above. While the chicken is cooking, heat the black beans in their juices.

Once the chicken is ready, place ¼ cup of the shredded cheese on top of each chicken breast and let stand in the open grill (or in the oven) for another minute, or just long enough for it to start melting. Remove the chicken from the grill (or oven) and place on plates. Top with the Cilantro Sauce and salsa. Serve with the black beans.

Ham and Winter Vegetable Potpie

3 tablespoons vegetable oil, divided
1½ pounds ham steak, deboned,
    trimmed of fat, and cubed
2 cups chopped onion
1 cup chopped celery
2 cups peeled and chopped carrots
2 cups peeled and chopped parsnips
3 medium peeled and chopped
    potatoes

1½ teaspoons dried thyme
Salt and pepper to taste
1 cup frozen peas
1 32-ounce carton chicken stock
1 9-inch Pillsbury premade
    piecrust*
2 tablespoons flour*
2 tablespoons butter*

Heat 1 tablespoon oil in a large pot over medium heat. Add the ham and brown the cubes all over. Remove the ham to a dish. Add the remaining 2 tablespoons of oil to the pan, and sauté the onion and the celery. Add the carrots, parsnips, potatoes, thyme, salt, and pepper. Stir to combine. Cook the vegetables, stirring occasionally, for 10 to 15 minutes, or until they soften. Add the peas, ham chunks and their juices, chicken stock, and stir. Cool the ham and vegetable mixture and freeze in an 8-cup container. Store the marked pie crust in the refrigerator.

To serve: Thaw the ham and vegetable mixture. About an hour before you want to eat, preheat the oven to 375°F. Take the 9-inch pie crust out of the fridge and allow it to come to room temperature, about 15 minutes.

Return the ham and vegetables back in the large pot and bring to a simmer. Melt the butter, then mix the flour into the butter. Stir the flour mixture into the ham mixture and simmer 5 minutes until mixture thickens slightly.

Pour the thickened ham and vegetable mixture into an 8-cup casserole dish. Unroll the piecrust and carefully put it on top of the casserole dish, sealing the edges to the dish firmly with your fingers. Cut a few slits in the top for ventilation. Place the casserole dish on a baking sheet and place it into the preheated oven. Bake for about 20 minutes, or until the crust is browned and the filling is bubbly.

SUMMARY OF PROCESSES: Debone, trim, and cube ham steak; chop 2 cups onions; chop 1 cup celery; peel and chop 2 cups carrots; chop 2 cups parsnips; chop 3 potatoes.

SERVES 4 to 5

FREEZE IN: 8-cup Ziploc freezer container

Spicy Korean Pork Barbecue

1 pound pork tenderloin, cut in
   ¼-inch slices
2 tablespoons brown sugar
2 tablespoons soy sauce
1½ tablespoons Thai chile
   paste

½ teaspoon ground ginger (or 1
   teaspoon grated fresh)
1 teaspoon dark sesame oil
½ teaspoon crushed red pepper
   flakes
1½ teaspoons chopped garlic

With kitchen shears, cut the tenderloin diagonally across grain into ¼-inch-thick slices. Combine the pork with the remaining ingredients in a labeled 1-gallon freezer bag and freeze.

To serve, thaw the pork and marinade and prepare a grill. Place a wire grilling basket on a grill rack. Remove the pork from bag; discard marinade. Place the pork on the grilling basket, coated with nonstick cooking spray. Grill 5 minutes turning frequently, or until you reach the desired doneness.

SUMMARY OF PROCESSES: Cut pork diagonally across grain into ¼-inch slices.

SERVES 4

FREEZE IN: 1 gallon Ziploc freezer bag

Pork Roast with Apples
and Mushrooms

1 tablespoon dried thyme
½ teaspoon salt
¼ teaspoon pepper
1 3- to 4-pound boneless pork loin
    roast

Sauce:
2 tablespoons butter★
½ cup apple juice
¾ cup chicken broth
¼ cup dry sherry

4 small cooking apples, peeled, cored,
    and cut into wedges (2 cups)★
2 cups sliced fresh mushrooms★

Combine the thyme, salt, and pepper. Package in a sandwich bag. Combine the sauce ingredients and package in a 1-quart bag. Place the pork loin roast (still in its store packaging) in a 1-gallon freezer bag, tuck in the bag of spices and the sauce bag, label, and freeze.

To serve, thaw the roast. Rub the roast with the thyme mixture. Place the roast on a rack in a shallow roasting pan and roast in a 325°F oven for 2 hours, or until the meat registers 160°F on a thermometer.

Transfer the meat to a platter and keep warm by tenting it with foil.

Meanwhile, in a large skillet melt the butter. Add the apple juice, chicken broth, and sherry, then add the apple wedges and cook and stir until golden. Remove the apple wedges from the skillet with a slotted spoon, reserving the pan juices; keep warm. In the same skillet, cook the mushrooms until tender.

To serve, place the slices of pork roast and apple wedges on individual plates. Spoon the mushroom sauce over meat.

SERVES 12 to 14

FREEZE IN: 1-gallon Ziploc freezer bag; 1 quart Ziploc freezer bag; 1 Ziploc sandwich bag

Penne in Cream Sauce with Sausage

1 tablespoon butter
1 tablespoon olive oil
2 cups sliced onion
2½ teaspoons chopped garlic
1 pound mild Italian sausage
½ pound hot Italian Sausage
⅔ cups dry white wine

1 14.5-ounce can diced tomatoes
1 cup whipping cream
½ cup chopped fresh parsley
Salt and pepper to taste
1 cup grated Parmesan cheese★
1 pound mini penne pasta★

Melt the butter with the oil in large skillet over medium-high heat. Add the onion and garlic and sauté until golden brown and tender, about 7 minutes. Add the sausage and sauté until golden brown and cooked through, breaking up the sausage as it cooks, about 7 minutes. Drain any excess fat from the skillet.

Add the wine to the skillet with drained meat and boil until almost all the liquid has evaporated, about 2 minutes. Add the tomatoes with their juices and simmer 3 minutes. Add the cream and simmer until the sauce thickens slightly, about 5 minutes. Stir in parsley and season to taste with salt and pepper. Cool, package in a labeled 1-gallon freezer container, and freeze with 1 cup Parmesan cheese in a sandwich bag attached.

To serve, thaw the meat sauce and simmer for 10 minutes, stirring frequently. Meanwhile, cook the pasta in large pot of boiling, salted water until tender but still firm to bite.

Pour the sauce over the pasta and sprinkle with Parmesan cheese.

SUMMARY OF PROCESSES: Slice 2 cups onions.

SERVES 6

FREEZE IN: 1-gallon Ziploc freezer bag; 1 Ziploc sandwich bag

Corn Soup with Basil, Avocado, and Crab

1 32-ounce carton chicken broth
3 tablespoons cornstarch
1 tablespoon butter
1 cup chopped onion
½ teaspoon chopped garlic
1 32-ounce package (4 cups) frozen
  corn kernels
1½ teaspoons salt

¼ teaspoon cayenne pepper
½ cup 2 percent reduced-fat milk★
½ cup half-and-half★
1 6-ounce can lump crabmeat, shell
  pieces removed★
1 peeled and chopped avocado★
1 tablespoon dried basil★
  (3 tablespoons fresh)

Combine the broth and cornstarch, stirring with a whisk. Melt the butter in a large saucepan over medium-high heat. Add the onion and sauté 3 minutes. Add the garlic; sauté 30 seconds. Stir in the broth mixture, corn, salt, and pepper and bring to a simmer. Cook 10 minutes, stirring frequently; do not boil. Cool the mixture, pour into a labeled 8-cup freezer container, and freeze. Store the remaining ingredients (★), marking the packaging.

To serve, thaw the corn mixture. Place half of corn mixture in blender, and process until smooth. Repeat the procedure with the remaining corn mixture unless you like a chunkier soup. Stir in the milk and half-and-half. Let stand 30 minutes at room temperature. Ladle soup into each of 4 bowls; top each serving with a spoonful of crabmeat, some chopped avocado, and a sprinkle of basil.

SUMMARY OF PROCESSES: Chop 1 cup onions.

SERVES 4

FREEZE IN: 8-cup Ziploc freezer container

Five-Cheese Spinach Quiche

1 16-ounce package chopped spinach, thawed, drained, and squeezed dry
4 slightly beaten eggs
6 ounces crumbled feta cheese
5 ounces crumbled Gorgonzola cheese
½ cup (2 ounces) shredded cheddar cheese
½ cup grated Parmesan cheese
1 cup (8 ounces) cottage cheese
½ cup chopped red bell pepper
1 cup chopped green onions
1 teaspoon salt
¼ teaspoon pepper
1 teaspoon dried tarragon
(1 tablespoon chopped fresh)

Combine all the ingredients in a large bowl. Spoon the mixture into a quiche dish prepared with nonstick cooking spray. Cover with heavy-duty aluminum foil, label, and freeze.

To serve, thaw the quiche. Preheat the oven to 350°F. Bake for 60 minutes, uncovered, or until set and lightly browned on top. Remove from the oven and let set for 10 minutes prior to serving.

SUMMARY OF PROCESSES: Thaw, drain, and squeeze dry package of frozen spinach; chop ½ cup red bell pepper; chop 1 cup green onions.

SERVES 6

FREEZE IN: 1 quiche dish; heavy-duty aluminum foil

Red Mesa Tacos

2 pounds lean ground beef
2 cups chopped onion
2 packages McCormick's chili
   seasoning mix
1 15-ounce can tomato sauce
1 14.5-ounce can diced tomatoes
2 15-ounce cans kidney beans
2 teaspoons chopped garlic
2 teaspoons sugar

1 teaspoon salt
1 teaspoon pepper
5 dashes Tabasco sauce
2 cups (8 ounces) shredded mild
   cheddar cheese★
1 package corn taco shells★
½ head chopped lettuce★
1 chopped tomato★
1 cup (8 ounces) sour cream★

In large pot, brown the beef with the onions and drain excess fat. Add the ingredients through the Tabasco sauce, and simmer for 30 minutes. Cool and package in a labeled 1-gallon freezer bag. Tape to this a sandwich bag fitted with the shredded cheddar cheese.

To serve, thaw the ingredients. Heat the taco mixture in a saucepan on stovetop over medium heat for 20 to 30 minutes. Meanwhile warm the taco shells. Top the tacos with the chili, cheese, lettuce, tomato, and sour cream.

SUMMARY OF PROCESSES: Chop 2 cups onion.

SERVES 9

FREEZE IN: 1-gallon Ziploc freezer bag; 1 Ziploc sandwich bag

Uptown Joes

2 pounds ground round
2 cups ketchup
½ cup Dijon mustard
½ cup Worcestershire sauce

½ cup sugar
½ cup packed brown sugar
6 to 8 hamburger buns ★

Brown the meat. Mix the remaining ingredients in small bowl, then add to the meat. Simmer 10 minutes. Pour into a labeled 1-quart freezer bag, and freeze. Freeze the hamburger buns.

To serve, thaw, heat, and serve on toasted buns.

SERVES 6 to 8

FREEZE IN: 1-quart Ziploc freezer bag

Peperoncini Pepper Roast

2½-pound chuck roast   1 16-ounce jar peperoncini peppers *
8 hard rolls *   Salt and pepper to taste *

Seal the roast in a labeled 1-gallon freezer bag and attach to it the hard rolls
in a second labeled 1-gallon freezer bag. Mark the jar of peppers to save.

When ready to serve, thaw the roast and rolls. Salt and pepper the roast and
place it in a slow cooker with the peperoncini peppers and their juice. Cook
on low for 8 hours. Pull out peppers and cut off the stems. Chop the peppers
finely and return to the sauce. Slice the roast, and serve on hard rolls. Use the
peperoncini sauce for dipping.

SERVES 8

FREEZE IN: 2 1-gallon Ziploc freezer bags

Orange Beef and Broccoli Stir Fry

1½ pounds flank steak
1 cup (8 ounces) orange marmalade
¼ cup hoisin sauce
3 tablespoons soy sauce

1 teaspoon chopped garlic
12 ounces fresh broccoli★
1½ cups uncooked rice★

With kitchen shears, cut the flank steak into ½-inch strips across the grain for stir-fry. In a small bowl, combine the steak with the remaining ingredients except for the broccoli and rice, label, and freeze.

To serve, thaw the ingredients. Cook the rice according to package directions. Cook the meat mixture in a wok over high heat until the meat reaches the desired doneness. Remove from wok and set aside. Cook the broccoli in the wok until crisp-tender. Combine the broccoli with the meat in a large serving bowl. Serve over cooked rice.

SUMMARY OF PROCESSES: Cut flank steak into ½-inch strips.

SERVES 4

FREEZE IN: 1-quart Ziploc freezer bag

ACKNOWLEDGMENTS

Thanks and hugs to all those who contributed to what is now *Once-A-Month Cooking Family Favorites*. We hope they comprehend how literally it is true that we couldn't have done this without them. What a joy it is to work on a great team!

Lori Baird—special diets consultant

Mary Leeper—research

Karen Seeling—special diets consultant

Nancy Student—Table Talk games

Julie Witte—proofreading (dozens of roses for Julie!)

Recipe Cycle Testers

Diane Arnett

Anne Gates

DaVinda Hsu

Kristi Moran

Donna Pease

Sharon Sulzle

Alice Tate

Missy Thedsord

Ruth White

Emily Davis

Dorothy Davis

Jeanette Davis

Korina Keller

Jeanna Lilleberg

Michelle Lingle

Heidi McCarthy

Becky Bartholomay Suko

Cathy Yarbrough

Sara and Kevin Wilson

Calvin Wilson and Alex Lagerborg
(our biggest, most patient taste
testers)

Recipe Contributors

Diane Arnett

Authumani/ Nancy Crane

Lori Baird

Nan Bertelson

DeLinda Blakemose

Tonya Blessing

Susan Carter

Carolyn Eumurian

Michael Flamini

Jacci Folk

Anne Gates

Sara Groves

Bob Hauck/ Kathleen Groom

Dorinda Jacobson

Heather Jansen

Peggy Lanum

Michelle Lingle

Lori Lundgren

Judy Miller

Kristi Moran

Jenn Myers

Barbi Odom

Jacquie Parella

Kathi Pitzer

Ginger Roerig

Shelly Steig

Zamie Stut

Nancy Sunderman

Alice Tate

Amy Wilson

Debbie Wilson

Kyndra Wilson

Lori Wilson

Sarah Wilson

Julie Witte

Measurements

2 medium carrots peeled and sliced=1 cup

3 medium stalks celery sliced=1 cup

1 medium green bell pepper chopped=1⅓ cup

1 medium red bell pepper chopped=1½ cup

1 medium zucchini=¾ cup chopped

1 large onion chopped=3 cups

1 medium onion chopped=2 cups

2 green onions chopped=¼ cup

1 teaspoon ground ginger=1 tablespoon fresh ginger

1 teaspoon dried spice=1 tablespoon fresh (generally)

1 medium boneless, skinless chicken breast half, chopped=1⅓ cups (un-cooked)

2 medium boneless, skinless chicken breast halves=1 pound [chicken breasts vary in size] 1 cooked, cubed breast=1 cup (may vary)

1 roasted (rotisserie) chicken, shredded=3 cups

1 pound lean ground beef or sausage browned and drained=2½ cups

1 pound cubed cooked ham=3 cups

16 ounces grated cheese=4 cups

Cheese packages: 6 ounce (some kinds), 8 ounces, 16 ounces

Olives: 1 6-ounce can yields 1 cup chopped olives

Rice: ¼ cup uncooked rice=1 serving

Chips: 1-ounce=1 serving (generally)

1 McCormick's Chili Seasoning Packet = 4T + ½ tsp.

8 tablespoons butter = ½ cup or 1 stick

1 fresh lemon yields 2–3 tablespoons juice

1 fresh lime yields 1½–2 tablespoons juice

¼ cup = 4 tablespoons

3 teaspoons = 1 tablespoon

16 tablespoons = 1 cup

8-ounces liquid = 1 cup

16-ounces liquid = 2 cups/1 pint

TABLE TALK

The meal is ready. The table is set. Family members all come to the table and sit in their usual places. Yes! That is quite an accomplishment. And the very routineness of the feat belies the tremendous significance of it, over time.

According to Miriam Weinstein, in her book *The Surprising Power of Family Meals*, research that has been accumulating from very disparate fields "shows how eating ordinary, average everyday supper with your family is strongly linked to lower incidence of bad outcomes such as teenage drug and alcohol use, and to good qualities like emotional stability. It correlates with kindergarteners being better prepared to learn to read. (It even trumps being read to.) Regular family supper helps keep asthmatic kids out of hospitals. It discourages both obesity and eating disorders. It supports your staying more connected to your extended family, your ethnic heritage, your community of faith. It will help children and families to be more resilient, reacting positively to those curves and arrows that life throws our way. It will certainly keep you better nourished. The things we are likely to discuss at the supper table anchor our children more firmly in the world. Of course eating together teaches manners both trivial and momentous, putting you in touch with the deeper springs of human relations."

Let's use Once-A-Month Cooking to help us to all that! But how can we promote an atmosphere of good conversation, above the chorus of chewing noises and the same-old talking about what happened at work today or which child misbehaved?

We like to, as we say, put a question on the table. The best of what we call Table Talk questions are those for which there is no right or wrong answer, and everyone at the table old enough to talk will have an answer. Once you get thinking this way, there is no end to the possibilities for conversation. Around the table we'll learn a lot about what is important to each of us. But we must agree that it's okay to disagree. No one's answer is "stupid." Here are some ideas to help you prime the pump.

Table-Talk Questions

For formal meals, it's fun to use place cards, writing a table talk question on the inside of each card. For more conversation starters, go to www.once-a-monthcooking.com.

For Anyone

What dream do you have that has not yet been fulfilled?

What is your favorite way to spend a Saturday morning? A Sunday afternoon?

Tell about a favorite place to which you've traveled and why you liked it.

Tell something about yourself that would surprise us—something that few people know.

Tell about a time when you were really scared.

Tell about a book that you have read that particularly affected you and how.

For Adults

Tell about a job you had before your current one and something you learned from it that has proved valuable.

Tell about a person who has mentored you, or whom you particularly respect.

What were you known for in high school? Is this trait or activity prevalent in your life today?

Tell about a significant turning point in your journey of faith.

What is a particular strength that you bring to your job?

Tell something positive and something difficult about your childhood.

Are you primarily an extrovert or an introvert? What do you do that recharges you?

What is one of your favorite movies and why did you like it?

If you had to live somewhere other than the United States, where would you live and what would you do?

For Passover

What are some other special foods we eat? On what occasion? Of what do they remind us?

Who do we know of that is in slavery now? What could we do to help bring them freedom?

What is something sad that you've experienced? How has that sad thing made room for something good?

What are some of the comforts you most enjoy?

(You'll find these questions and more at http://www.happypassover.net/4-questions.html)

For Easter Dinner

If you had been present at Jesus' Last Supper with his disciples, what question would you have asked him?

For Thanksgiving Dinner

Finish this sentence: Thanksgiving wouldn't be complete without _____.

What difficulty have you faced in the past year for which you are thankful?

Where is one place you've gone this year that you were thankful to be?

What is a good memory from this year?

What is your favorite food on a Thanksgiving plate? What favorite food are you looking forward to at Christmas, Hanukkah or Kwanza?

For Christmas Dinner

Tell us about a favorite Christmas ornament.

What is your favorite Christmas tradition?

If you could give one special gift to the person on your right, and money was no object, what would it be?

If you had been there in the stable, what is something you might have heard Mary and Joseph say to each other?

What is your earliest Christmas memory?

What do you look forward to at Christmas besides presents?

What did you like best about a particular past Christmas?

Whom do you see yourself as most like in the Christmas story?

What has been the best about this Christmas season?

Tell about a Christmas season that was particularly hard for you.

What is something you're looking forward to in the New Year?

Other Conversation Starters

Our friend Nancy's family plays the **Guessing Game** with their young children. Whoever suggests they play the Guessing Game goes first, unless they choose to give their turn to another. Not everyone at the table has to choose to play, but Nancy's found that even if people don't choose at first, they're usually in the game by the end.

The person who starts thinks of a person, place, or thing. Other players shout out questions: what color is it? What sound does it make? Does it live in our state?

If someone thinks she knows the answer, she can shout it out. If it's wrong, they keep going. If it's right, that person can begin the game anew. They don't keep score. They're all winners!

The Guessing Game is fun when they have company at the table. For a child eating with a family they don't know, it's a great way for him to get involved in conversation. He doesn't have to talk about himself.

The **Topic Game** is a spin-off of the Guessing Game. Whoever goes first picks a topic. They go around the table and ask each person a question about the topic. For example, if the topic is fruit, questions may be like Mommy, what are your three favorite fruits? Damien, name four fruits. Once they have gone around the table, it's the next person's turn to start a new topic.

At the table is a significant place to build family identity, security, and those warm memories that years later keep us coming back home, both in our thoughts and for visits.

ADDITIONAL RESOURCES

For downloadable tools such as Shopping Lists and Menu Charts, an E-Newsletter, and helpful tips from other Once-A-Month cooks, visit www.once-a-monthcooking.com.

Index

DINNERTIME NOTES

DINNERTIME NOTES

DINNERTIME NOTES

DINNERTIME NOTES

DINNERTIME NOTES

DINNERTIME NOTES

DINNERTIME NOTES

DINNERTIME NOTES

DINNERTIME NOTES